THE
WORK AND PLAY
OF WINNICOTT

THE
WORK AND PLAY
OF WINNICOTT

Simon A. Grolnick, M.D.

Jason Aronson, Inc.
Northvale, New Jersey
London

Library of Congress Cataloging-in-Publication Data

Grolnick, Simon A., 1930–
   The work and play of Winnicott / Simon A. Grolnick.
     p.   cm.
   Includes bibliographical references.
   ISBN 0-87668-802-4
   1. Child analysis. 2. Psychoanalysis. 3. Winnicott, D. W.
(Donald Woods), 1896–1971. I. Title
RJ504.2.G76 1990
155.4—dc20   89-18572
                                                   CIP

Manufactured in the United States of America. Jason Aronson Inc. offers books and cassettes. For information and catalog write to Jason Aronson Inc., 230 Livingston Street, Northvale, New Jersey 07647.

To my wife and four daughters

Contents

Preface

After living in a more or less Winnicottian-colored world for the last eighteen years, it is not easy to not (Donald Winnicott loved double negatives) write a Winnicottian-colored preface in a Winnicottian manner. Winnicott gave us a long-needed permission to play, and to interplay, form and content. Prefacing the specter of a book is an awesome enterprise—will the book that was in me look at me and feed back what I am and have become during these years? Will my Winnicott be an imitation of him or, at least in part, the record of an interplay between his ideas and imagery and me? Some of the answers I must find out myself and some must be left to my readers.

One wouldn't show a very Winnicottian bent if my major acknowledgment was not to my patients. For it was not my teachers, but my mixing of patients, Winnicott's writings, and observing my wife Maxine's mothering relationship with my four daughters that served to teach and inspire me. More specifically, I thank my patients for being patient with me, and tolerating the patient in me, for telling me when I was wrong, for regressing far, far back and away from me, for giving me the chance to become angry, even enraged, and forcing me to deal with and assimilate that rage. I thank my patients for hiding in almost impossible-to-create corners in my office, and I want to thank my historical "patient," Emily Dickinson, whom I "met" in Amherst and in her poems, and with whom I played in a paper or two. In a Derridean sense, she knew much more about Winnicott than I ever will. I thank my adult patients who still sucked on grown-up thumbs and held on to quite adult stuffed animals. I thank my patients for revealing to me the gaps in their experience, their histories, their early development, and their relationships with others and with me. Without these gaps, there would have been no impetus to bridge missing structure and meanings or to want to traverse those bridges not alone, which in turn has led to the desire to understand and write about these matters and share them with my co-workers and players.

I am indebted to my colleague and friend, Werner Muensterberger, who introduced me to object relations theory when I was a candidate at the then Downstate Psychoanalytic Institute (now the Psychoanalytic Institute at New York University). This was in the early 1960s and American psychoanalysis was not ready for terms such as *dual unity,* which Werner was not hesitant to introduce to us. His paper, "The Creative Process: Its Relation to Object Loss and Fetishism," influenced me greatly and was one of my meaningful introductions to Winnicott. Werner's inspiration, advice, and aid in contacting and negotiating with the European Winnicottians was critical in helping Leonard Barkin and myself put together *Between Reality and Fantasy: Transitional Objects and Phenomena.* My deep thanks to my co-editor and colleague, Leonard Barkin, who helped me think out the meta- and ego-psychological implications of Winnicott's work. Clare Winnicott became a witty, dedicated counselor and, while she lived, was a vital link to the Winnicott tradition. Others who served as crucial transitional figures between classical psychoanalysis and Winnicott were Susan Deri, Judith Kestenberg, Anni Bergman, Martin Weich, and Gilbert Rose. Jason Aronson went out of his way to provide support and wise advice throughout the lengthy process of putting the book together. And then I will never forget the encouragement I felt from André Green, who, after sitting through a Winnicottian-oriented paper I delivered at the American Psychoanalytic Association meetings in the early 1970s, came up to me and earnestly asked me how come an American was so interested and involved in Winnicott. My greatest thanks goes to my wife Maxine, who as a partner and colleague, listened to me for endless Winnicottian hours and helped me to work out the ideas in this book. I also want to express my gratitude to Stefanie Turnbull, Nicolette Gersten, and Peggy Baldinger, who helped prepare the manuscript and gave me needed encouragement during difficult times.

In a half-serious, half-playful manner, I want to *un*acknowledge a number of colleagues and teachers who looked on me as a not-quite-Freudian anomaly, an upstart, and perhaps (I never can be quite sure) as a metapsychological misfit. I forgive them—they didn't stop me, they provided a reality that resisted, that I could bounce ideas off, and I know they were chained with the bonds of orthodox theory that sometimes allows little movement. It was the inspiration of some creative and open colleagues and a few teachers (Leon Altman was one) that enabled me to use these discouragements and put-downs in a positive manner. But above all, it was Winnicott's writings that helped me understand the tough going involved in learning to use the object, in this case, theory. He has helped us all to use theory and not allow it to use us.

1

Why
Winnicott
Now?

What accounts for the growing interest in the work of England's quixotic pediatrician–psychoanalyst?

An admittedly oversimplified answer is that Winnicott was the master of the middle, the in-between. Winnicott turned compromise and conflict into paradox, paradox that dances between the polarities within modern thought in psychoanalysis and its related fields. Because his ideas can be applied to these existing polarities, Winnicott is causing excitement in both child and adult psychoanalysis, and in aesthetic criticism, anthropology, and intellectual thought in general.

First let us look at psychoanalysis. Winnicott's ideas were probably conceived while he was observing babies as a pediatrician, but those ideas saw the light of day when he was an adult and child psychoanalyst. Contemporary psychoanalysis is caught between a still mechanistically tinged ego psychological, structural model (ego, superego, and id) and self psychology that includes a self that Kohut (1971), the father of self psychology, refused to define. The conceptual level around which self psychology hovers is close to that of the fleshing out of the so-called object world that is being accomplished in the work of the object relational school. This includes not only the experience of and the actuality of the object, but the experience of and the actuality of the relationship between both the inner and outer self and objects. Psychoanalytic developmentalists attempt to fill in the gap that has arisen as the natural science, oedipal level structural model strains to meet the needs of the widening diagnostic entities encountered in our consultation rooms. Margaret Mahler's developmental view (Mahler et al. 1975) of separation–individuation has been helpful. Then Otto Kernberg (1975) has used Mahler and Jacobson's (1964) work on the self and object worlds to attempt a comprehensive bridge between structural drive theory and self and object relations theory.

While Mahler and Kernberg and others (Greenberg and Mitchell 1983) have helped to cantilever the sometimes all too distant shores of psychoanalytic theory, their ideas are not easily translatable into the art of interpretation. It is here that we are beginning to use Winnicott. He is the modern theorist who manages to integrate the polar differences into a good enough, comprehensive schema of development that does translate into and naturally facilitate the three worlds of theory, technique, and the application of psychoanalysis to related disciplines. Winnicott's scientific imaginative world lends itself best to what could be called a poetics of interpretation that takes into account the innovativeness of man, the symbolic animal, as well as his constitutionally and biologically driven nature.

Winnicott provides a kind of transcendent middle for the use of play in child therapy and psychoanalysis. On one side, Melanie Kleinian play therapy was modeled after the associationist, and virtually textual, nature of the use of free associations in adult analysis. Here the therapist reads the semiotics of play as if *verbal* content was involved. Kleinian-influenced interpretations often dove to a level that seemed to talk to a silent unconscious. On the other hand, starting with the surface, ego psychological child therapy derived from Anna Freud took defenses into account to such an extent that sometimes the line between education and interpretation became fuzzy. Winnicott saw the world of both children and adults in strong developmental terms, with play as one of development's favorite media. Play meant something, but it also *was* something. It can be said that Winnicottian play therapy combines meaning and developmental interaction where content and form interweave and become more one during play. Play involves gesture and the body as well as the symbolic world. So Winnicottian play *means,* while at the same time facilitating, development.

In the intellectual and academic world, there has been an alleged return to Freud (Schneiderman 1980), principally through the contributions of Jacques Lacan (1977). The rallying call was "the unconscious is structured as a language." Ego psychology became a repressive enemy and ego began to have political, suppressive overtones. However, the word *id* is not exactly a lexical lion, and it surely does not roar. Patients began to be treated too much as texts. At the same time, in the world of aesthetics, literature, linguistics, and anthropology, a hermeneutic or subjectivist reader or audience response interpretation dominated the critical journals and the classroom. The world of the work of art belonged to the reader or the viewer and no longer to the author. Play was present, but a play subsumed under the deconstructionism of Jacques Derrida (1974) that came closer and closer to becoming a solipsistic exercise. Thus, while psychoanalysts became afraid of the hermeneuts in their midst, literary critics began to feel that their own interpretive attitude was making them dizzy. As Winnicott's ideas gradually became more public during the past decade, they became known in psychoanalysis's related fields. Winnicott's system plays back and forth (using play itself as a medium) between the body and the mind, between the inner and the outer, between the more basic and the more sophisticated.

Self psychological and hermeneutic views of psychoanalysis also began to cry out for the reality of a fundamental bodily and gestural foundation, while the more biologically, causally minded American ego psychological movement cried out for a less structured, more imaginative theoretical milieu from which the therapist can construct an interpretation. Winnicott's work, which gradually grew from his observations of children to his ultimate assumption (in his nonassuming manner) of the intellectual leadership of the middle, object relational school of British psychoanalysis, offers a solution in the form of developmental line and an interactional frame of reference that still remains within the rubric of Freudian psychoanalysis, that is, unconsciousness, preconsciousness, transference, countertransference, resistance, aggression, and sexuality are all very much taken into account.

Winnicott knew his ideas were important in fields outside the province of his own discipline. However, the intellectual, aesthetic, and psychoanalytic worlds were not ripe for them during the time he was alive. Others have carried his ideas further than he did. At this point in time, the creativity and profundity of his view of the world deserve continued consideration; now many more seem ready for it.

The obvious danger present with the arrival of any new body of ideas is that they become fashionable and the surface of the ideas is mistaken for the substance. In Winnicott's instance, since the ideas are at the same time disarmingly commonsensical, yet quite complex, it would be most ironic but very possible for this to occur. This book is dedicated to presenting the reader with basic, in-depth knowledge of Winnicott's thinking and its more recent elaborations, so that the reader will pursue his writings directly and thus acquire the essence of the rich legacy he has left us.

2

The Man
and the Analyst

PERSONAL HISTORY

Marion Milner (1978), one of Winnicott's co-workers, tells us in a memoir that Winnicott once said to a student just before a lecture, "What you get out of me you will have to pick out of chaos." An exaggeration (Winnicott was prone to that vice), but there is some truth to it. Winnicott was a lot of things; many feel he was a genius. He was an old-fashioned, hands-on pediatrician at heart, and yet he thrived on the intrapsychic world of the psychoanalyst. The work of geniuses can be difficult. He was an artist and knew of the poetic use of language. He wove his unique ideas and his evocative words throughout his many writings. In some ways the reader can start in the middle or the end, as well as the beginning. Ideas are refined, worked over, left behind, and inevitably returned to later on. He experienced and wrote within the intermediate world of the imagination, and like a kind of psychoanalytic Tolkien, he mapped out this intermediate world that psychoanalysis had never conceptualized adequately.

However, Winnicott's chaos was not without form. The inter-woven ideas were never fully organized in a comprehensive manner, except in a few papers in which he presented a more linear and discursive version of his unfolding developmental schemata. This book presents the personal, professional, psychoanalytic, and intellectual sources of his stimulating, and at times startling, contributions, describes the essence of those ideas, and then shows how they can be used as helpful guidelines for the therapist.

It should be said that by using Winnicottian concepts one cannot show a therapist *how* to say it and *when* to say it. But actually Winnicott was a therapist's therapist. Reading him helps free up one's natural therapeutic verve that too often is squelched by an all too rigid cleaving to arbitrary rules. Winnicott often referred to the stultifying effects of pedantic teachers and their pedantic texts, how these created a lack of authenticity and served as the gravediggers of our creative sources. The same for teachy parents who sadly pontificate with their potentially open and creative offspring.

Thus, one part of Winnicott thrived on immersing himself in the imagination and working from instinctive and intuitive sources. The "facticity" of life seemed to annoy him; he preferred to soar. It is of this Winnicott his wife and co-worker, Clare Winnicott, wrote almost a decade before her death. Winnicott was a proud Devonian and was aware that there was a town on the detailed map of Devon called Winnicott. Clare Winnicott commented (1978), "We never actually found the village, although we always meant to. It was enough that it was there." Winnicott's map of the mind was not just a bland schema of ego psychology, but a vivid, populated, liveable, emotionally authentic land that both a patient and a therapist must indwell to enable a therapy to occur that reaches the guts and the bones.

However, to reassure the reader who fears the encouragement of wild analysis, there was another Winnicott, one who took copious notes, who read the scientific and medical literature, and who insisted on intellectual rigor. He lived out his belief that originality must spring from a steady base of tradition and organization. Winnicott spent his life trying to show his readers, his students, and his patients how being traditional and straight does not preclude being startlingly novel. It was one of many paradoxes that are so difficult for most of us to entertain that seemed to have come so naturally to this English gentleman whom many described as a "pixie" or a "bit of a Peter Pan" (Grosskurth 1986, p. 399).

The question arises: What were the historical, cultural, and psychological factors that helped to form this quixotic man of science? The challenge then is to understand Winnicott's family and social origins. But Winnicott, as with all psychoanalysts, had two families, personal and psychoanalytic. In a field where psychoanalytic genealogies search for linkages with Freud the Father, and where one's personality and one's ultimate psychoanalytic political fate are sometimes determined by one's analyst, one's second family can vie for importance with the first. But now chronology must win out. A short biographical sketch should be helpful to explain this to the reader.

Donald Woods Winnicott was born in 1896 in provincial Devon, Plymouth. It is clear that he lacked very little. His father was a well-to-do merchant who had sufficient time and idealism to be knighted for the civic contributions he made, and he was a political animal who became mayor of Plymouth. While there is not much biographical information readily available about Donald's mother, his second wife, Clare (1978), wrote that Donald's mother was "vivacious and outgoing and was able to show and express her feelings easily." Sir Frederick was apparently dignified and poised, and he possessed high intelligence, solid judgment, and a good sense of humor, the latter quality which he shared with his wife.

Winnicott had two older sisters, five and six years older than he. Sometimes he felt like an only child, was lonely, and used to find a special tree of his own in whose branches he did his homework. He also haunted the kitchen and spent a great deal of time with the cook. What this meant we may never know, but the situation does lend itself to speculation. The family was traditional in that Sir Frederick's elder brother, Richard, lived across the road with his wife and Donald's three male and two female cousins. As Clare Winnicott (1978) wrote, "There was never a shortage of play-mates. . . . There was always something to do—and a place to do it in, and someone to do it with if needed." It is most interesting that this biographical material, while at times approaching a mythology of a happy, thriving extended family, did contain elements of the future Winnicott personality and style. While he loved to work with patients, related well to children as a combined Mother Goose and Pied Piper, and involved himself socially and politically, many described him as basically a loner and sometimes difficult. His low-keyed position as the leader of the middle school was a marked contrast to the leadership styles of Anna Freud and Melanie Klein, who were the nominal heads of the competing schools in the British Psychoanalytic Institute. Winnicott's ultimate interest in the world of the imagination, his existential leanings, the Rousseauistic liberalism, and his almost political desires to free the True Self, as he called it, from the tyranny of the dominating demands of the False Self, seem to have sprung de nouveau from his family background. However, the family model of poise, dignity, and a basic decency and seriousness did seem to establish a dialectic with the capacity to play, laugh, and live heartily. Somehow, whether through some dissonance in early attunements or a golden birthright of creative genes, there was a continual need to create into absence, absence in himself and in his patients. In an at present nonpublished autobiographical fragment (entitled *Not Less Than Everything*) referred to by Clare Winnicott (1978), he prayed, "Oh God! May I be alive when I die." He and Emily Dickinson ("I heard a fly buzz when I died") shared a lot, fought traditionalism while living within it, and constructed psychological systems of their own to cope with existential anxiety, a private metaphysical system in the case of the female poet, and a unique and original psychoanalytic poetics in the case of the male psychiatrist. And it is not insignificant that both were childless. But Emily would lower baskets of cookies from her second-story bedroom window to the neighborhood children, and Donald played with and emotionally touched literally thousands of children, many of them victims of the war and of deprivation in all of its forms.

Ultimately the story of Winnicott's early life and its influence on his adult personality may be told when someone attempts a needed definitive biography. But let us move on with some of the landmarks of his life. Winnicott attended the Leys School in Cambridge when he was 14. At 15 he broke his collarbone, and in a reparative resolution he decided that ultimately he wanted to enter medical school. His first impulses were to practice the kind of medicine one might have expected he would practice: general, family medicine. He pursued his premedical studies at Jesus College in Cambridge. At the same time, he was a voracious reader of literature and continued to refine his appetite for music, tending to be interested particularly in Bach, and as the dark shadows of chronic lung and heart disease eventually began to restrict him, the dark and transcendent tones of Beethoven's quartets. As a young man in college, he rented a piano and entertained his fellow students with his playing and a fine tenor voice.

Winnicott pursued his medical studies at the Cambridge colleges at the beginning of the First World War. Some of his friends from college had gone into the front lines and were killed in action early in the war. Though Winnicott was deferred as a medical student, he felt guilty and decided to enter the fray. He chose the navy as a medical orderly, demonstrating the antielitism and the willingness to throw himself into the jaws of danger to deal with his guilt and allow an outlet for his idealism. Later on, those jaws took the form of what he called the "unthinkable anxieties" and the suicidal crises of the sometimes hopeless patients he taught himself to treat.

When the war was over, he continued his medical studies at Saint Bartholomew's Hospital, where he entered the front lines of the blood and guts of big city medicine. Then he was subjected to what seemed to be a major formative experience: he developed a lung abscess and found himself a patient among the very patients he had ministered to as a physician. Clare Winnicott (1978) reports that a friend who knew him at the time heard him say that he was convinced that "every doctor ought to have been once in his life in a hospital bed." It is not hard to relate this to Winnicott's subsequent deep interest in countertransference and to his adherence to the belief prevalent in British psychoanalysis of a basic psychotic core in everyone—helpers as well as helped. In addition, his own patient-hood combined with large doses of empathy, survival guilt, and his medical background sensitized him to psychosomatic aliveness or to deadness and its developmental origins, which relates to his concept of the true and false self.

In medical school, Winnicott became interested in his dreams and read a book by Oscar Pfister, the Swiss cleric who had obtained psychoanalytic training. Soon Winnicott began to think of obtaining training in psychoanalysis; for pragmatic reasons he decided he would stay in London in order to undergo a personal psychoanalysis. His keen interest in children and in developmental processes led him to train to be a consultant in children's medicine; at that time there was no official specialty of pediatrics. He joined the staff at the Queens Hospital for Children and at Paddington Green Children's Hospital. It was at the latter that he spent forty years converting the clinic (which he referred to as his Psychiatric Snack Bar) from a purely medical clinic to one that leaned heavily in a child psychiatry direction. Clare Winnicott (1978) writes about how he never saw a child without giving him or her something to take away after the visit. It was usually something as menial as a piece of paper he had folded into the form of a fan or an airplane and played with for a moment before handing it to the child.

Winnicott's career was shaped intensely by the events in Britain during the Second World War. He was appointed as a consultant to the Evacuation Project and spent his time supervising workers at hostels used for children who manifested too much delinquency to allow them to be placed with families. It is here that he realized how much environment contributed to delinquent action (the antisocial tendency) and how much underlying deprivation was at the source of this tendency. It is here that he realized how interpretation must be accompanied by careful attention to the environment and how important holding and handling and a good enough setting were for normal development to take place, or for there to be a chance for the correction of abnormal development. Also, it was here that Winnicott met psychiatric social worker Clare Britton, who was, in 1951, to become his second wife. Winnicott's first marriage, one that began when he was 28, had been unsuccessful. Apparently his first wife suffered from significant psychiatric disturbance (1978, personal communication, Clare Winnicott), but Winnicott loyally remained with her for many years until he was able to break away. The marriage to Clare was an excellent one; they shared their work and ideas, and both knew how to play together. During one of her visits to New York before she died in 1984, Clare delighted in telling me about how often she and Donald would end up a period of playfulness by playing on the floor together. (This playfulness and seeing play as a form and method of treatment was borne out when a colleague of mine, Werner Muensterberger [1976, personal communication] met Winnicott for a first supervisory session. Winnicott ambiguously asked him where the patient was. When his supervisee asked him what he meant, Winnicott enquired whether the patient was on the couch, in the chair, or on the floor!) As a corollary, Clare Winnicott told me that when Donald Winnicott was once asked whether a particular frequency of visits was compatible with doing a psychoanalysis, he answered with something like, "It depends on who's doing it." For Winnicott, the process was in the mind of the analyst, not in the ironically more behavioral criteria of where the patient was or how frequently the patient was being seen.

THE PSYCHOANALYTIC CLIMATE

Winnicott's "intermediate stance" seemed to be a product of his constant predilection for dialectic encounters. The psychoanalytic battlefield in England was an ideal setting to promote this process. The principal struggle was between the schools of Anna Freud and Melanie Klein. Anna Freud, of course, carried on her father's classical psychoanalysis into its newer version, ego psychology. The stress was on a deterministic mental apparatus, but the need to take into account the ego, its relationship to the id and reality, and the complex development of the superego tended to humanize an originally mechanistic model of the mind. Anna Freud promoted analyzing from upward down, and the metaphors for leaping to the nether regions that characterized the earlier phase of id analysis gave way to (somewhat mixed) metaphors such as that of peeling the layers off the onion. In child analysis, Anna Freud was cautious and spent time supporting the child and respecting his or her defenses. Interpretations were made from ego, defensive, and adaptive standpoints.

It may be more than a bit ironic that Melanie Klein was the polar star opposite the controlled, conservative, never married Anna Freud (although she had a long, probably platonic relationship with Dorothy Burlingham, with whom she lived) (Young-Bruehl 1988). Klein (Grosskurth 1986) as a young woman was eccentric, hearty, a dancer till dawn, and attractive. Her psychoanalysis was more id-oriented, went for the gut, and stressed the death instinct. It is also ironic that Klein migrated from Berlin (she had been born in Vienna but was trained and analyzed by Ferenczi in Budapest) in 1926 and hence preceded by twelve years the Freuds' arrival in England. Klein's migration followed a successful series of six lectures (ultimately published as *Psycho-analysis of Children* [1932]) that were given in the London home of psychoanalyst Adrian Stephen, the brother of Virginia Woolf. Woolf, incidentally, with her husband Leonard, was the owner of The Hogarth Press, which published most of the psychoanalytic writing in England as well as the Freud Standard Edition. James and Alix Strachey, the latter of whom befriended Klein during their analysis with an ill Karl Abraham in Berlin, and Ernest Jones all thought the brilliant young woman would add a zesty intellectual ingredient to the somewhat stuffy London psychoanalytic environment. But it cannot be forgotten that Jones also wanted Klein to treat his children.

Winnicott landed right in the heart of this colorful cast of characters. In 1923 he initiated what turned out to be a literal decade of analysis with James Strachey. What happened between these two interesting people can only be guessed. Strachey, who as a young man had been homosexual, had an unconsummated infatuation with the handsome English poet Rupert Brooke and was the brother of the bohemian homosexual biographer Lytton Strachey. James was a card-carrying member of the Bloomsbury group, and a fair amount of the early information about him comes from the diaries and letters of his friend Virginia Woolf. But it doesn't seem to be this side of James Strachey that Winnicott knew. Strachey is characterized later on as having been somewhat forbidding, and Lytton Strachey's biographer, Michael Holroyd (1973), describes an interview with an aging James Strachey, who was isolated and wearing a Sigmund Freud beard that rendered him a virtual look-alike. This is the same James Strachey about whom there is a controversy concerning his and Alix's translation of the Standard Edition. Some claim, among them Bettelheim (1983), Mahony (1982), and Ornston (1985), that the Stracheys took the soul and the flesh out of Freud, anglicizing and bowdlerizing him to boot. Others still feel that the Standard Edition is a masterpiece. But clearly Strachey, a creative, brilliant man, devoted most of his literary life to being someone's translator, and not a creator. How he dealt with this Freud transference in the countertransference with his patients, one can only speculate. Some of this is hinted at in his letters to Alix when she was in Berlin during her analysis with Abraham (Meisel and Kendrick 1985). An excerpt from a letter dated London, October 9, 1924, is perhaps all too typical:

> I'm beginning to doubt whether Dr. W.'ll *ever* stump up. He finally sent an order to someone to sell something out. And the reply was

that the signature didn't stimm with the original signature when the things were bought. He thinks he vaguely remembers or he imagines it's possible, that his father signed his name for him. But *I* think he's altered his writing on purpose to make further delays. Meanwhile at any moment the Rates may be due and all lost.

Referring to another occasion, in a November 3 letter, Strachey is still concerned about paying the rent and very aware that he has only two analytic patients, Winnicott and a man who had just started and is referred to as 'Enery. After mentioning 'Enery, he goes on: "But the other gent is awfully leisurely. And though he got another nice bill on Saturday, and though he had a most suitable dream last night, there wasn't a sign today of his intending to pay it. (I told him a month ago that I wanted him to stump up each time.)" On other occasions, in a similar anecdotal manner, Strachey described the details of this patient's sexual fantasies, seemingly partly for the edification of but as much for the amusement of his absent wife.

From the Strachey letters, one cannot help but be skeptical as to the success of Winnicott's analysis with Strachey. Strachey may have tried to hide his countertransference behind technique. It seems more than coincidental that Winnicott spent so much time with the true and false self concept and always warned about the dangers of false self analysis, known as intellectualized analyses.

Strachey was influenced by Klein to some extent, and he tended to be one of her defenders. In his famous paper, "On the Nature of the Therapeutic Action of Psychoanalysis" (1934), he used object relations theory. But he never was deeply involved with the Klein who insisted on the sadistic death instinct, an earlier and earlier placing of the Oedipus complex, and the kind of "sky diving" id analysis she practiced with patients who often seemed bewildered at her interpretations. (Rycroft [1985] referred to transcripts of these analyses as Pinteresque.)

However, the vitality of Klein's personality and ideas attracted

Winnicott. In 1935, a year after he finished his Strachey analysis, Winnicott started a six-year supervision with Melanie Klein. Grosskurth (1986) reports that Klein (who had analyzed and written about her analyses of her own children) had wanted *him* to analyze one of her children and be his supervisor. With good sense, he refused, took on the analysis, but did not talk at all about it with Klein.

Winnicott's "romance" with Klein continued when several years after he terminated with Strachey (and certainly during his supervision with Klein), he began analysis with one of her more colorful followers, Joan Riviere. Riviere had been analyzed by Jones in 1916, thereby becoming the first lay analyst in England. (Klein and Anna Freud were never physicians, and Strachey left medical school after a very short trial—quite a contrast to D. W. Winnicott, M.D.) Riviere came from English upper-class intelligentsia and learned German expertly during a year of education in that country. She was interested in language and was one of Freud's official translators, working under Strachey for a period of time.

Riviere was, like Klein, a most controversial figure. She lost her faith in Freud, somehow, after he developed his cancer, and she used to attack him in print. Freud fought her back, and even used her as an effigy to vent his spleen against Klein. So it must have been Winnicott's intrigue with Riviere's brilliance, her being one of "queen" Klein's retinue, her interest in language (and his masochism?) that led to her choice as his second analyst.

Now that many Winnicott letters are available (Rodman 1987), the mystery can be cleared up a bit. A long November 17, 1952, letter to Klein is most revealing. Its background is that the Joan Riviere introduction to the volume *Developments in Psychoanalysis* (from which Winnicott had been excluded because of a critical footnote he wrote in his paper on transitional objects) maintained that Klein had produced an all-inclusive, comprehensive theory of development under which all others could be subsumed. Then, almost two weeks earlier, Winnicott had read a paper at the psychoanalytic society entitled "Anxiety Associated with Insecurity."

It is clear that the paper was either criticized or translated into Kleinian terms. In the letter Winnicott stressed the need for theoretical language to be alive. He wrote to Klein (Rodman 1987, p. 34), "I personally think that it is very important that your work should be restated by people discovering in their own way and presenting what they discover in their own language. It is this way that the language will be kept alive." He criticized a Kleinian analyst for having bandied about a lot of "Kleinian stuff" without "having an appreciation of the processes personal to the patient. One felt that if he were growing a daffodil, he would think he was making the daffodil out of a bulb instead of enabling the bulb to develop into a daffodil by good enough nurture." Here was Winnicott at his best, taking on the tyranny of a dominating transference and language and selling facilitation to the heathen. Here was Winnicott living out his developmental beliefs in the hot arena of British psychoanalytic politics. I sense that letter-writing was a way for him to aggressively assert himself, but that he was so injured in personal encounters that he had to sheath his sword.

But Winnicott, earlier in the letter, referred to his two analyses:

> What I was wanting on Friday undoubtedly was that there should be some move from your direction towards the gesture that I make in this paper. It is a creative gesture and I cannot make any relationship through this gesture except if someone came to meet it. I think that I was wanting something which I have no right to expect from your group, and it is really of the nature of a therapeutic act, something which I could not get in either of my two long analyses, although I got so much else. There is no doubt that my criticism of Mrs. Riviere was not only a straightforward criticism based on objective observation but also it was coloured by the fact that it was just exactly here that her analysis failed with me. [p. 34]

So there it was—Winnicott implied, within the context of the letter and the immediate events that preceded it, that his analyses were not liberating and that he felt constricted by a prison of theory and language. He implied that his theoretical orientation was pushed by attempts to undo and master the years of dead time he spent in analysis. (Yes, you *learn* so much else in analysis, as Winnicott mentioned, but he was primarily interested in helping people to live meaningful, hopefully happy lives.) That his writings and experiences as an analyst and therapist were continuing attempts at completing his own analysis is crystal clear. But this also provides the hope for his readers that doing therapy is therapeutic. He writes as if he wished his readers and students did not have to do it the hard way, as he did.

As we learn more and more about Winnicott's inner life, it becomes clearer where he fits in the twentieth-century psychoanalytic scene. He was able to take the best from psychoanalytic ego psychology, the best from the object relations aspect of Kleinian psychoanalysis, and the best from his own creative wellsprings; in a humanistic, existential, political, personal, and professional life campaign, he forged an original system of thinking about human development and the repair of its imperfections that is well worth mining.

Winnicott's last years were bittersweet. Chronic lung disease (he smoked too much) and heart disease limited him, but he pushed on to finish as much of his mission as he could. In November 1968, I heard him give a talk at the Downstate Psychoanalytic Institute; he seemed chipper and alert. A short time later, he was invited to present a paper at the New York Psychoanalytic Society, the beachhead of European psychoanalysis in America. Winnicott chose a paper that is now considered one of his best and most influential, "The Use of an Object and Relating through Identifications" (Winnicott 1971e). It was discussed by three conservative members of the society and then by the general audience. In spite of the fact that Winnicott was an invited guest, the paper was attacked strongly by most discussants. I was told by his wife Clare and other analysts in England that he was quite taken aback and hurt by what had happened. In addition, he had not been well. A day or two later he

developed heart failure and had to remain in Lenox Hill Hospital for
almost two weeks before he could leave for England. Clare says he
never stopped feeling upset about the entire visit.

Winnicott struggled with his illness but continued to work with
patients and ideas to the end. When he died, his dedicated spouse
devoted the rest of her life to seeing that his letters, notes, clinical
records, and unpublished papers would be made available to psychoanalysts, other mental health professionals, child psychiatrists,
pediatricians, and scholars. She eventually set up a Winnicott Trust
in England, which oversaw the publication of his writings and
decided to place the originals of Winnicott's letters and records in
the History of Psychiatry Library (the Diethelm Library) at Payne
Whitney Clinic, which is part of the Cornell University Medical
College. She thought that here the Winnicott material would be
most available to physicians, particularly pediatricians, people in
the mental health field, and academic scholars. Clare Winnicott
spoke of Winnicott's vision that his ideas might be helpful to psychoanalysts, workers with children, and academic scholars in fields
such as sociology, anthropology, linguistics, philosophy, and literary criticism.

3

Winnicottian Principles

W innicott left us with a comprehensive system that is a most original contribution. He was a unique man and perforce a unique psychoanalyst. In keeping with his own natural antipathy to describe and nail down his patients into artificially diagnostic compartments, his ideas defy neat categorization. Winnicott's theorizing and his technical innovations intersect with traditional Freudian conflict theory, Kleinian theory, object relational theory, existential therapy, logotherapy, family therapy, and even sociotherapy. Basically Winnicott didn't care in which section of the encyclopedia he would be inscribed. But all this presents a challenge to the author and, since we live in a reciprocal world, to the reader. After providing some hints about reading Winnicott, I think it would now be helpful to introduce some of the overriding, basic principles that inform Winnicott's work. In doing so, I will indulge a little in the tempting enterprise of utilizing some of the terms that have become a part of our psychotherapeutic language. The good enough mother, the holding environment, the transitional object, and the true and the false self, for example, have been used as headings to organize discussions of Winnicott's ideas. In succeeding chapters, however, I will present his ideas from the standpoint of what I perceive to be the interweaving series of developmental lines that he traced out, many for the first time. However, this should aid the cause of therapeutic applicability. In anticipation of these chapters, I think the reader would benefit from knowledge of Winnicott's basic principles, including a sprinkling of his evocative phrases. Some of these principles are psychological, some are philosophical, and some existential in nature; some are ideas, and others are stances and attitudes.

WINNICOTT'S "TOTAL PERSON"

Winnicott, like many who reacted against a mechanistic, structural psychoanalytic theory, was concerned about the "ghost in the machine" (Koestler 1967). Winnicott tended to see his patients as people, or persons, as he preferred it. He epitomized this when he talked of how it is possible to cure a neurosis and yet still leave an essentially unhappy person. Blandness and conformity were anathemas to him. To this creative man who wandered into medicine and psychoanalysis, a symptom-free person with no spark of life, no authenticity or originality was tantamount to a dead person. He was concerned not with the sepulchral but with the living person, the whole person. His principles help us to visualize the development of an authentic individual and how that development can go awry, and if unfortunately it does not occur optimally, how we can use the therapeutic situation to repair the damage. Winnicott didn't merely take the theoretical absence of the self into account in theory, but rather in the very nature of the psychoanalytic situation itself.

WINNICOTT'S "NATURAL PERSON"

Winnicott, the master of paradox, believed in a kind of primal innocence, even though he was alert to aggression, sadism, and the evil of domination. His infant, as we shall see, was Rousseauistic in essence, and, in keeping with Freud, it was civilization, childrearing, and education that turned the original into a rubber stamp copy. This romantic side of Winnicott found difficulty with Melanie Klein's more evil and death-instinctual baby, thereby stimulating a dialectic that continued through most of his career, until he ultimately tried to rid himself of the ghosts of Freud and Klein.

But the word *natural* refers to nature, and Winnicott, with his medical and traditional side, could not close his ears to the call of the flesh. The second major collection of his papers, and what is probably the major statement of his work, is entitled *The Maturational Processes and the Facilitating Environment* (1965). Although Winnicott principally staked out the environmental side in the nature–nurture continuum, he never failed to take into account the effect of biology, the genes, and the drives. In addition, his work precedes the psychobiological and psychopharmacological explosion. It is now necessary to integrate the new information we have on the regressive illnesses, such as depression and schizophrenia, and use Winnicott's schemata to understand and treat the more psychological side of development. Winnicott's theoretical and technical guidelines clearly are not geared to the neurotransmitter (although the work of Kandel [1978] and others show how environmental influences can change the neurochemical matrix). Winnicott helps us to see and conceptualize how, in health, the psyche "indwells" the representational soma with a reasonable fit. If there is a dissociation of the psyche and soma, there is danger of depersonalization, or a psychosomatic expression of needs and meanings. With the benefit of the reader's editing and updating, Winnicott can be approached in a more modernist manner concerning his basic faith in our potential for happiness and creative living, but the soma that he referred to must now be seen in a more complex manner.

Winnicott didn't think mothers could be taught to be optimal in their childrearing. But here is the paradox. Without her *own* optimal mothering, how can a mother be an empathic, developmentally tuned creature? Here Winnicott can help us out by reminding us that mothers cannot be conceptualized without babies, and the empathic and stimulating effects of the baby on the mother help to evoke (perhaps better than any therapist) her authentic caretaking capacities.

WINNICOTT'S DEVELOPMENTAL STANCE

Winnicott was a radical developmentalist. He saw development in the traditional manner, as an interaction between those aspects of constitutionally determined tendencies that are interactive with the environment. For Winnicott, development proceeded in a natural manner and required an optimal milieu in which to occur. Parents cannot be prime movers of development; they can only facilitate it by providing steadiness, love, empathy, enough frustration, and impact with reality and aggression. It is this model of the unfolding of optimal early development that serves the therapist well when deciding how to help our developmentally disabled patients. While Winnicott was clear that one cannot make a direct parallel between development in the child and the adult, for him certain similarities did exist. The therapist provides the *setting* (an important Winnicott word) for a new developmental phase (Loewald 1960) to occur, and the patient is faced not only with an interpreter of insight but someone who can hopefully provide him with a new developmental experience.

The key concept in modern psychoanalytic developmentalism is *internalization*. Functions that were provided by the caretaker are, through countless numbers of interactions with the child, gradually and increasingly internalized, becoming self-evocative (Fraiberg 1969) intrapsychic structure. The comforting, holding mother, for example, is gradually placed "inside" and carries on her essential work, at first in an imagistic, introjective manner and later in a more abstracted, "metabolized" manner. Internalization is gradual and can be conceptualized in terms of developmental lines. As we shall see, Winnicott's internalization is never completed. It is constantly in equilibrium with externalizing processes. This has allowed the post-Winnicottians to evolve the concept of the *transitional process* (Rose 1978, 1980), in which there is a continuous interaction between inner and outer, between perception and fantasy, and between primary process and secondary process.

Winnicott's developmental unfolding is not linear but spiral in nature. Progression is almost invariably followed by temporary regression that is not pathological but rather provides a resting place, a return to home base that, for example, is built into Mahler and colleagues' (1975) rapprochement phase. This spiral model is not original with Winnicott; it was an intrinsic part of the developmental schemata of Hans Werner (Werner and Kaplan 1963) and, from a more neuropsychological standpoint, Gesell (1954).

WINNICOTT'S VIEWS ON DEPENDENCY AND REGRESSION

The Winnicottian therapist is in a dilemma. He or she is trying to meet the dependent and regressive needs of the patient. Yet at the same time, no patient, no matter how depressed or schizophrenic, is in the same psychological state as an infant. This is all made more complex by the fact that child observational studies by Stern (1985) and others show that there are wired-in capacities to differentiate self and other and to arrive at certain correlations between various sensory modalities. Thus, even the classically dependent infant is not a totally dependent creature. Nevertheless, both caretakers of infants and Winnicottian therapists should be tolerant of the dependent and, importantly, regressive needs of their respective charges. It is here that Winnicott's *holding environment* becomes a crucial concept. When the infant requires external support in both a literal and figurative sense, the adaptive externalization of the caretaker's originally internalized holding takes place and the capacity to *hold* is passed on intergenerationally. Winnicott spells this out in his paper "The Theory of the Parent-Infant Relationship" (1960d):

> It includes the whole routine of care throughout the day and night, and it is not the same with any two infants because it is part of the infant, and no two infants are alike. Also it follows the minute day-to-day changes belonging to the infant's growth and development, both physical and psychological. [p. 49]

Winnicott felt that this holding was necessary for the patient to experience some sense of continuity, a *going-on-being* feeling, as he put it. It is when there is a sense that one is held; that there is a safety net present rather than the hard concrete of the circus floor; that one won't be dropped, physically or metaphorically; that one can experience one's self, and *be* one's self. Winnicott prescribed *being* before *doing,* for action that feels authentic and not merely acting must take place from the platform of a sense of stability and continuity.

Holding also protects the infant, and the patient, from *impingement,* a traumatic disruption of the sense of continuity occurring when the individual is not ready to encompass this disruption. Impingement must be differentiated from developmentally necessary frustration, the crucible out of which the life-sustaining process of internalization can occur.

GOOD ENOUGH CARETAKING

Winnicott's concept of the *good enough mother* is probably his best-known contribution. What did he mean? It is such a broad concept that it lends itself to distortion. Did Winnicott help to establish a *good enough* standard that can be interpreted as leaning toward the very mediocrity he despised? I do not think so. Good enough mothers, while always present to some degree, replace a more constant, empathically flexible holding environment. Mothers begin to move from the phase of *primary maternal preoccupation* (Winnicott 1956b), where they are almost totally involved with their recently newborn infants. The mother comes to her senses and realizes that she also is a person with needs and with a pleasure principle of her own. The infant's cry and the mother's responses are no longer virtually simultaneous. The phase that Winnicott called *primary creativity* has passed, that is, the mother's biological and psychological ability to present the breast or an object to the infant so the infant has the (implied) *illusion* that he or she omnipotently created that object, providing a primordial sense of effectiveness and the ability to have impact. The necessity for relatively constant omnipotence, or the sense of symbiosis, to provide primitive ongoingness and a core of fullness to the self must give way to a holding environment that is disturbed by mistuned and mistimed moves on the caretaker's part. What Winnicott called optimal *ego relatedness* ("the type of relationship that exists between an infant and the ego-supportive mother") must be mixed with optimal frustration, which is necessary for ego building. Winnicott's thinking here is similar to Freud's ego, which was built of identifications with the lost object, and in turn, with Kohut's mini-identifications with raged-against and mourned objects, a process he called *transmuting internalization.* So the good enough mother (or, really, caretaker) empathically gratifies and, in fine paradoxical Winnicottian manner, deceptively but helpfully frustrates—but only to the degree that impingement and trauma do not occur. The good enough mother implies that she settles for a good enough child, and the Winnicott model of therapy implies a *good enough therapist* treating a *good enough patient.* Winnicott equated the perfect and the saccharine with developmental destructiveness.

WINNICOTTIAN AUTHENTICITY

For Winnicott, the sense of feeling real, feeling in touch with others and with one's own body and its processes was essential for living a life. This is most epitomized in his concepts of the *true and the false self* (Winnicott 1965). (This is clearly a developmental line that will be traced out more fully in Chapter 5.) Briefly, if the infant and child can feel supported but not directed and dominated, there is a chance for the expression of an inner sensorimotor, gut self. But this must be preceded by enough *mirroring* (Winnicott 1971b) experience, in which the caretaker has given the child the validation of inner experience. Repeated distorted parental mirroring behavior forces the infant into an acceptance of someone else's view and the possible beginning of a future false self formation. The pathological entity of a false self, which at the extreme could become an as-if personality, is in a continuum with the falseness that is necessary for the social ability and minidiplomacy required in everyday living.

Winnicott was wary of the *false self analysis* or *therapy*. This all too common state of affairs occurs when there is a collusion between the intellectualized aspects of both the patient and the therapist (the false self frequently utilizes the defense of intellectualization). Two people can do therapy together and virtually never (metaphorically) touch each other. The chance to authenticate the self is lost and, in fact, there is a reinforcement of a dissociated and/or isolated mode of experiencing on the patient's part. Concomitantly, in such treatment situations the therapist cannot grow in a true developmental sense.

WINNICOTT'S POSITION ON CREATIVITY

Overriding all of Winnicott's contributions is the concept of *creativity*. Life without creativity is not authentic. Psychic death occurs without a sense of experiencing the innovative and the new. It should be stressed here that Winnicott was not talking of the artist's or the genius's creativity, but the creativity of everyday life. He is referring to the capacity of every man to be able to view and experience the world in original, even aesthetic terms. So Winnicott doesn't attempt to explain artistic creativity. Believing in a Rousseauistic baby, he describes the necessary but not sufficient conditions that *facilitate* (a crucial word for him) the individual's natural creativity. To take a creative leap, or even a little skip, off the beaten track, one must feel that the base of operation is a stable one, that experience has been continuous enough to tolerate the risk of discontinuity. In closer to adult terms, Winnicott explained that to be innovative or different, one must have a traditional position to start with, so that there is a continuous dialectic between the conventional, the safe and secure, and the creative.

This is a sound developmental principle, aside from its educational implications for enhancing creative potential. Trial and error is a must for progression to occur. This relates to the spiral model of development referred to above—progression must give way to the stabilizing and refueling of a regressive position. The child must be able to try and err, and to feel that the errors will be appreciated almost as much as the successes. Concomitantly, a patient in a healthy therapeutic environment should feel free to err and potentially displease the therapist. And it is possible for the therapist to feel ultimately pleased at the patient's feeling free enough to make mistakes and be errant enough to aggress against the therapist. Thus, reciprocal Winnicottian therapy model stresses the need for a therapist to feel free to be wrong, to try out interpretations or even the therapist's own associations with the patient, who, if not in a submissive stance toward a dominating, pedantic therapist, can try out the interpretation for size and turn it away if it doesn't fit. Of course, what is implied here is the achievement of a state of affairs that may *in itself* be a major goal and achievement of therapy and not only a method.

Thus for Winnicott creativity is thought of as natural, as necessary, as capable of bringing a fullness and joy of living, as being part of both the developmental process and the therapeutic process. It can't be taught, but must be *facilitated* in children, in patients, and in therapists.

PLAYING, PARADOX, AND ILLUSION

Winnicott's most lasting contribution was his description and eluci-
dation of the concepts behind transitional objects and phenomena.
The transitional object is the first part self–part mother, a part
self–part objective reality, the first possession that is imbued in an
animistic act with qualities of the self and of the other. It is the
ancestor of the intermediate mental space of the imagination and of
the symbolic world that so epitomizes the human animal. As Winnicott said it, it is our first illusion, and a me-not me experience that
represents the beginning of the developmental line of the ability to
maintain *paradox*.

Clearly Winnicott was tuned in to a crucial aspect of human
experience that generally psychoanalysis had addressed only tan-
gentially. Living too much in the concreteness of factual reality is no
better for the reasonably adjusted and happy human than living in
fantasy. Successful living occurs *between* reality and fantasy (Grolnick et al. 1978) in the "illusory" world. Winnicott used the word
illusion in a different sense than it had been used in classical
academic psychology, where it referred to a false perception based
on an inner experience projected onto a kernel of reality (e.g.,
seeing an intruder in the shadows of the corner of a room). For the
word *illusion* is derived from the Latin *ludere*, which means "to
play." If any of us were not able to have the illusion that all was well,
to play at feeling and acting as if the world and we would go on
forever, as if we and our loved ones would not end as dust, it would
be hard to go on, and the reverberating circuits of existential angst
might turn us all into creatures shrieking on a Munchian bridge.
Man must play. There seems to be an evolutionary, adaptive,
built-in capacity to play, what some have dared to call a play
instinct. Many have contributed to an ever increasingly sophisticated literature on play as a philosophical, evolutionary, developmental, psychological, and aesthetic phenomenon, for example,
Rousseau (1762), Schiller (1795), Groos (1910), Huizinga (1955),

Cassirer (1944), Callois (1958), and Bruner and colleagues (1976). For a while, this literature tended to equate the innovativeness of play with creativity itself. Cassirer (1944) reminded us that play was a necessary but not sufficient aspect of art, and it is this principle to which Winnicott adhered. As referred to in the section on creativity, Winnicott was interested in enhancing the creative potential of the man in the street: being able to play, to play within one's own imagination, to be able to play with others, to play while working, and to play when making love ("foreplay" is a term that recognizes this) all protect us from a no-play dullness that, to Winnicott, again, was premature death.

For those who might misinterpret Winnicott (who often leaves himself open to misinterpretation because of his very playfulness and capacity for ambiguity), the play he prescribes for adults is strongly related to the old homily that play is the work of children. Winnicott's *playing,* an action concept, is *developmental play.* Play in childhood and throughout the life cycle helps to relieve the tension of living, helps to prepare for the serious and sometimes the deadly (e.g., war games), helps define and redefine the boundaries between ourselves and others, helps give us a fuller sense of our own personal and bodily being. Playing provides a trying out ground for proceeding onward, and it enhances drive satisfaction. Judith Kestenberg (1971) points out that as the infant is feeding from the breast or bottle, little infant hands play with the mother's clothing, rubbing and patting, touching and letting go. It is the first instance of play for its own sake, and, as Kestenberg writes, it is play that is an *adjunct* to drive satisfaction. This adjunctive role continues until later on when play can become autonomous. Winnicott repeatedly stressed that when playing becomes too drive-infested and excited, it loses its creative growth-building capability and begins to move toward loss of control or a fetishistic rigidity. At normative levels, the free play of the nursery during latency gives way to the more rule-oriented play of games. Civilization's demands for controlled, socialized behavior gradually, and sometimes insidiously, supersedes the psychosomatic and aesthetic pleasures of open system play. Hopefully the basic core of more innovative spontaneous play can still persist in the social, territorial, and even recreational games in which, by definition, we all become involved. Then the progressive capacity to regress can sometimes allow even highly social and traditional adaptors to return to the playful delights of nursery experience.

It is exactly this area that Winnicott applies to the therapeutic situation. André Green (1978) reminds us that one of Freud's favorite metaphors for the analytic situation was that of the chess game, with its prescribed rules. Classical psychoanalysis is set up as an experimental, closed system, with an objectively directed aim in mind. (Many of us consider this system to be obsolete.) This is in contrast with a Winnicottian therapeutic rubric, which includes ample opportunity for play *for its own sake.* As a corollary, if the patient cannot play, then the necessary conditions that enable a kind of backtracking of the developmental position of the patient must be established. After all, how free can association or communication be if the patient has used the language of the talking cure in a rigid, imprisoned manner since childhood? The *squiggle game* is Winnicott's technical gift to us all. The patient or therapist makes a line, and the other party continues, and so on, until the two construct a picture that is created out of their combined imaginative processes. This model that Winnicott used for diagnostic and therapeutic reasons (1971d) can be applied to language—*transitional language* as it has been called (Weich 1968, 1978)—where the analyst's verbal images become the counterparts for the lines of the squiggle game. This specific technique will be elaborated on in Chapter 8.

WINNICOTT AND GENERAL SYSTEM THEORY

Winnicott's way of looking at development and how the psyche relates to its soma and its surround is compatible with von Bertalanffy's (1933) general system theory, even though Winnicott never directly cited this important contribution. Winnicott was interested in living organisms and did not appreciate an artificial, dualistic separation between baby and mother, psyche and soma, past and present. He disclaimed a purely deterministic view of mental processes and felt that the therapeutic situation should allow for and promote uninte- grated times (Winnicott 1958) where the concept of meaninglessness becomes possible. He felt that for novel, creative responses to occur, there must be a steady backdrop of a holding environment. These innovative, creative responses seem to be imbued with a sense of free will and spontaneity. Here, essentially, the chemical equation model for the closed system way of looking at the analytic or ther- apeutic situation is replaced by an open system, much like that sug- gested by von Bertalanffy (1933). That object relations theory is a general system way of looking at one aspect of the mind has already been pointed out by Sutherland (1980).

Winnicott's transitional object, for example, travels a long, varied Odyssean voyage through the course of development. It begins with sensorimotor, attachment levels, moves toward the imagistic, intro- jective level and then, hopefully, through the more abstract, sym- bolic level. Each interface is in some continuum and equilibrium with both sides even though, as more developmental advance occurs, the hierarchal level of the interfacing qualities shifts. The system is open- ended, and new energies emerge. All kinds of play, ranging from nursery play to games to the play of the theater—where the actors and the director and playwright, and at another level, the actor and the audience—are in a reciprocal interplay with one another. This series of reciprocalities and the analogy of the theater and the ther- apeutic situation have been elaborated on by Loewald (1975), Pedder (1977), Grolnick (1984), and McDougall (1982).

WINNICOTT, FAMILY THERAPY, AND THE PSYCHOLOGY OF GROUPS

That Winnicott thought in general system terms and that he was deeply interested in family interactions render the bridge from his work to that of family therapy a short one. The link between object relations theory and family therapy has been best described by Slipp (1984). Slipp finds the holding environment a congenial concept and refers to Khan's (1974) inclusion of caretaking functions of the *family* as part of the basic holding environment. Slipp goes on:

> We can further suggest that the family be viewed as a natural extension of the original symbiotic oneness with mother. The family is the mother group that normally provides the security and strength (a holding environment and a transitional group) to facilitate the child's individuation and separation from the family and adaptation in society. [p. 86]

Since Winnicott was a major force in freeing psychoanalysis from its preoccupation with the nearly exclusive study of the intrapsychic world by bringing the environment, both representational and real, into psychoanalytic theorization, it is not difficult to extend his ideas into an understanding of socialization and cultural processes. Family therapists, cultural anthropologists, and sociologists have been increasingly interested in his work. It should be remembered, however, that Winnicott's concept is developmental in nature, that it takes the individual into account. Empathy, creativity, and good enough caretaking are intrinsic to this system. Already, as is inevitable, misapplications of his ideas are beginning to occur (see Chapter 11). For example, therapists and organizations are attempting behaviorally to create transitional objects for children's use to compensate for maternal loss or deprivation. This ignores Winnicott's premise that the transitional object is created when the developmental balance is just right and the mother is able to present an object to the child just at the special moment that object is desired. The unchallenged illusion is one of the child having created the object himself, thus leading to the sense of possession of an object that is endowed with loved qualities derived from both the self and the mother. This is a far cry from the clumsy attempt of giving a transitional object to a child and expecting it to be accepted naturally by the child.

4

The Winnicottian Mother-and-Baby

I do not believe in the story of Romulus and Remus, much as I respect wolf bitches. Someone who was human found and cared for the founders of Rome, if indeed we are to allow any truth at all to this myth. [Winnicott 1966, pp. 9–10]

It is possible to seduce a baby into feeding and into the functioning of all the bodily processes, but the baby does not feel these things as an experience unless it is built on a quantity of simple being which is enough to establish the self that is eventually a person. [Winnicott 1966, p. 12]

I once risked the remark, "There is no such thing as a baby"— meaning that if you set out to describe a baby, you will find you are describing a *baby and someone*. A baby cannot exist alone, but is essentially part of a relationship. [Winnicott 1964b, p. 88]

A BABY AND SOMEONE

It is important to consider the essence of Winnicott's system, its very foundation. Clearly, that is the *mother* and the *baby*. And as is evident, the mother and the baby cannot be conceptually separated. Winnicott calls them the *nursing couple*. He apologizes to fathers about this but feels that fathers have their compensations and have a crucial role in protecting the nursing couple from adversity.

In object relations theory, which Winnicott essentially works within, the principal interest is in the internal representation of the self and the other. More recently, it involves primarily the internalized *relationship* between the self and the other. Of course, this includes the results of identifications within objects and identifications within the projections of the self onto objects. Because the principal units of structure are self and object images, or in a more advanced sense, representations, and not the more depersonalized units of structural theory (ego, id, and superego), there is more of a tendency to take the actuality of the *interpersonal* world into account. We are now at a time when psychoanalysts of a Freudian bent and those of an interpersonal, Sullivanian persuasion are beginning to meet more in the middle.

But Winnicott adds another dimension to object relations theory, almost by definition. He is concerned with the mother–infant couple, the relationship between them, and because relationship (for the infant) at an early time is expressed and experienced so much in terms of space and boundaries rather than anything more sophisticated, we must include the space, both literal and metaphorical, between them. In another sense, paradoxically there is a triangulation present within the dyad, although it may be conceptualized as a potential in the beginning. The intermediate space is characterized by some sense of separateness, even from day one (as baby watchers Stern [1985] and others have taught us). Thus, the transactions within this space (interactions, exchanges, objects, etc.) can be seen as me-not me entities. This is also so with the very (Euclidian) space itself (Bergman 1978).

It is in this "third" or "intermediate" world that transitional objects and phenomena, and ultimately third parties, appear. In process terms (transitional process [Rose 1978]), this intermediate world is filled with the interplay of inner and outer experiences, that is, between fantasy and perception (including perceptions of the body), between self and nonself, and between primary and secondary process thinking. It is in this in-between, interplay world that our imaginative, symbolic life can grow.

Thus it can be said that the Winnicottian mother–child unit is a dynamic, alive, interactive unit that is there to do more than just meet the biological needs of both parties, such as the good "feedings" of the satisfactions of good mothering and the sucking and full stomach needs of the child. The unit is a potential creator of a child who has developed a solid fundamental base upon which to build a vibrant personality that is capable of pleasure, love, and playfulness. This is a developmental line that is vital to Winnicott's view of the formation of the personality (see Chapter 7).

The real or "outer" actors in this play during child rearing cannot, of course, be artificially separated, if we are Winnicottian, from their internal representation and the internal representations of others who possibly preceded them or who are simultaneous surrogate caretakers. But it is acceptable within the theory to speak of the real mother and the real infant. They do not have to be operatively placed aside, as they are to a greater extent in a more classical ego psychoanalytic system. The caricature of this was a well-meaning comment of one of my first psychoanalytic supervisors. When I brought in some information about what I thought were the destructive effects of an angry narcissistic mother and how these effects were reflected in the patient's fantasy life, my supervisor mused that no matter who our families are, the imagination creates its own neurotic fantasies independently. Retrospectively, I think I would now say to him that if the family setting is originally facilitating enough, and a solid foundation of being is first built, *then* the child is free to create his or her own original fantasies that, in some sense, can transcend his or her origins. Without that foundation, the ego is split or fragmented, and neurotic fantasies are only effluvia.

A WINNICOTTIAN MOTHER

Winnicott had great faith in the natural ability of mothers to mother. He was concerned that this talent not be damaged, much as the art educator is concerned that a pedantic art instructor can dwarf the creative potential in a gifted student. Sometimes Winnicott even reflected that some mothers might be better off not being taught anything about mothering, as it only makes them self-conscious and more clumsy in their "mothercraft," as he once put it. In the end he entertained and clearly practiced the belief that it *is* better for mothers to know about mothering, even though they can't be taught how to do it. His reasoning was that knowing about the natural processes of mothering and how they unfold provides a body of knowledge that the mother can use to ward off more arbitrary, rote advice on how to be a good mother, thus enabling her to "fight for her rights," as Winnicott stated it.

Winnicott's terms, *the ordinary devoted mother* and *the good enough mother,* do in themselves help to create an open, tolerant-enough environment so that the mother is more likely to feel free enough to be herself. This includes the ability to be able to commit mistakes and use that necessary condition of trial and error to arrive at a reasonably right developmental tuning. Winnicott spells out again and again that the initial time of *primary maternal preoccupation,* where the infant becomes the center (but clearly not everything, as there usually are other members of the family), helps the mother meet the infant's need more or less on time. When the mother decenters the infant and begins to feel for her own and the rest of the family's wants, the phase of gradual disillusionment that is necessary for the building of the inner self and the object world and some optimal separateness–togetherness for that particular setting can begin. In addition, Winnicott stresses to the mother (1987, p. 19) "how necessary it is for you, in your turn, to have a space to yourself." Virginia Woolf couldn't have said it better.

LEARNING TO MOTHER

However, there is a paradox built into Winnicott's nondidactic instructions. While "good enough" implies the absence of an imperative to be perfect, the concept of *optimal* (I used that word in the previous paragraph) is virtually unavoidable. Winnicott writes (1964b, p. 87), "Can we not say that the mother *adapts herself* to what the baby can understand, actively adapts to needs? This active adaptation is just what is essential for the infant's emotional growth. . . ." It is difficult not to turn this good enough, tolerant ideal into one where the good enough combination of gratification and meeting needs, along with frustration and misalliance, starts to become an ideal in itself. Winnicott is aware of this danger. He wrote (1966, p. 13), "Sometimes mothers find it alarming to think that what they are doing is so important and in that case it is better not to tell them." But he did feel that most mothers instinctively know how important mothering is and that a knowledge of the imperfections that are part of the process is more liberating than oppressive.

ONCE UPON A TIME

There is another Winnicottian principle involved in the enlightenment of mothers. This involves Winnicott the psychoanalyst, in that psychoanalysis is the uncovering of a reasonably plausible history of an individual's growth and development. Winnicott (1964d) comments, "People want to know about the beginnings of their lives, and I think they ought to want to know. It could be said that there is something missing in human society if children grow up and become in their turn fathers and mothers, but do not know and acknowledge just what their mothers did for them at the start" (pp. 9–10). He goes on to explain that he doesn't mean that he is encouraging children to thank their parents for creating them and

raising them: "I am trying to draw attention to the immense contribution to the individual and to society which the ordinary good
mother with her husband in support makes at the beginning, and
which she does *simply through being devoted to her infant*" (p. 10).

Winnicott was a narratologist, a consummate storyteller who
also was a cryptic believer in narrative theory. He believed that
man is a storytelling animal. Much modern literary criticism empha-
sizes this. But so did Erikson (1950) even more manifestly than
Winnicott. We all want to know about what happened "once upon a
time." The end of the day, the time for nighttime rituals, is the time
Western society places children in their own private rooms and uses
the bedtime fairy tale to tell of the beginnings, the middles, and the
ends to help carry the child through the absence and darkness of the
night. Winnicott brought all this right into his developmental
schema. A mother who has a sense of history will tend to have a feel
for both personal and generational history and will possess a need
to pass on this sense of continuity to her children.

However, Winnicott offers us (both parents and therapists) *more*
than the general knowledge of Eriksonian life history and literary
critical narrative theory that are built in to our thinking (we probably all feel that a cohesive individual is held together in part by a
sense of and knowledge of life and family history). But Winnicott
goes directly to the base of narrative capacity. This can be seen
more directly in his fairly well-known paper (1941), "The Observation of Infants in a Set Situation." Here Winnicott devised a set
observational situation. He writes that he would "place a right-
angled shining tongue depressor at the edge of the table and invite
the mother to place the child in such a way that, if the child should
wish to handle the spatula, it is possible." He saw much of the
mother–child interaction in this arrangement. It is most interesting
that many children reached for the spatula, hesitated for just a
moment, looking around to see mother's reaction, and then took
the fascinating object with the kind of satisfaction that looked to
Winnicott as if the child had imaginatively swallowed the object.

But the observer's eye was equally on the mother. Here he was most interested in seeing whether the mother could allow the entire sequence to play itself out. He wrote on this later on: "For one thing, we have witnessed a completed experience. Because of the controlled circumstances there could be a beginning, a middle and an end to what happened; there was a total happening. *This is good for the baby.* When you are in a hurry, or are harassed, you cannot allow for total happenings, and your baby is the poorer" (1964a, p. 77).

Thus, Winnicott stressed the need to provide the child with a "strong sense of start and finish." I think Winnicott was working here on the developmental line of narrative, and showing that our ability to play out life's story with its beginnings, middles, and endings is enhanced when there is a parent who has enough of a sense of *history* to allow narrative sequences, at first primitive and later more symbolic, to play themselves out. The implications for the therapist are obvious. Winnicott referred to this in the "Set Situation" paper and followed up throughout his later writings. The patient cannot be told his story, but must be allowed to develop it and sequence it in his or her own time and place. The therapist (and, analogously, mothering figure for the child) provides the setting and the boundaries. Stories must have form and structure, but to be alive, they must be free at the same time. The reader might be interested in a more cognitive, but still quite related, study of the developmental line of narrative as described in an informative book, *The Child's Concept of Story: Ages Two to Seventeen,* by Arthur Applebee (1978).

THE WINNICOTTIAN MOTHER—A PRÉCIS

As the picture of a Winnicottian mother unfolds, she is seen as empathic but still concerned with self. She is desirous of providing pleasure and play for her child but knows that the tragic side of life requires boundaries, restrictions, frustrations, and graded disillusionments. Hopefully she can wait, can sit back, can be a facilitator, can absorb the aggressive affects of the child; yet she knows when she has to step in and take over, and if necessary, "end the session." Therapists please note! Incidentally, Winnicott seems to imply that good mothers would make the best therapists. But that *he* is reported to have been a superb, sensitive, and ingenious therapist with children, belies this implication.

THE WINNICOTTIAN BABY

The naive critic of the Winnicott world view not too infrequently begins to assume that it includes an infant who is constructed purely out of mother love and empathy. This is just not true. In a lecture to mothers entitled "The Baby as a Person" (1964a), Winnicott wrote, "Mothers have no difficulty in seeing the person in their own babies from the start" (page 79). Here he was going somewhat against the current of psychoanalytic thinking, which tended to see, at least with the first few months, a relatively undifferentiated stage, later refined more as the symbiotic phase in Mahler and colleagues' (1975) schema of development. But Winnicott recognized this little person with maturational lines was ready to go. He conceptualized what we can only think of as an inborn capacity for playing that serves as the base for the developmental line of imaginative thinking, his "third" or "intermediate" world. He wrote:

> Who can say how early there are the beginnings of this imaginative life of the infant, which enriches and is enriched by the bodily experience? At three months a baby may want to put a finger on mother's breast, playing at feeding her, while taking milk at the breast. And what about the earlier weeks? Who knows? A tiny baby may want to suck a fist or finger, while taking from breast or bottle (having cake *and* eating it, so to speak), and this shows there is something more than just a need for the satisfaction of hunger. [1964a, p. 79]

David Levy in the 1940s demonstrated that there are sucking needs over and above the biological or drive needs involved in eating. But even though Levy was a child analyst and very much interested in play, I don't think he conceptualized the early adjuncts (Kestenberg 1978) to drive satisfaction as play precursors.

Thus in this area, the Winnicottian baby is not all too different from the Sternian baby (Stern 1985), the latter having wired-in capacities for discrimination from day one, far from an "undifferentiated" primal mental apparatus. However, one of the differences is revealed by Winnicott's offhanded "Who knows?" in the above paragraph. Winnicott arrived at his conclusions and speculations from the careful observation of infants, children, and adults. But they were not within the methodical, controlled experimental conditions set up by Stern, Emde, Sander, and others. I do think that the two bodies of knowledge will ultimately prove compatible, with the reservation that Winnicott's observational level conclusions and theories are subject to the usual revision necessary for any scientific work.

BABIES AND DEVELOPMENT

General psychoanalytic theory of development (including Winnicott's) conceptualizes that the developmental aspects of growth occur as a complex interaction between intrinsic maturational processes and the priming, facilitating, and maintaining effects of a generally supportive environment. The external support at first substitutes for not yet materialized psychological functions, which then are gradually internalized into the ego of the infant-growing-into-child. When the caretaking environment lets the infant down, or "drops" him or her (as Winnicott liked to put it), the infant is at the mercy of his automatically unfolding constitutional (including drive) processes. A "person," or the process of *personalization,* cannot occur naturally, and if there is not Winnicott's sine qua non of reciprocity, there is a danger that the person and the sense of a somatic self are dissociated, with the concomitant possibility of a *false self* formation and/or psychosomatic illness rather than a more optimal *psychosomatic indwelling* in which some of the sense of the flesh and its anchoring reality is imbued within the sense of the personality. Sometimes these infants can be spotted early. They laugh *heartily* and cry in a "gutsy" manner. And as is shown in the latest infant observation studies, whether the system "clicks in" depends on the variables of the wavelengths of the infant and those of the caretakers—how they harmonize or create cacophony together. It cannot be emphasized enough that the harmony I refer to is not that of elevator music but more the harmony of a Beethoven quartet or some of Schoenberg's middle work. There must be a "harmony" of the aggressive dialogue, which includes a bending and a willingness to be destroyed (metaphorically) but a capacity to always survive in the eyes of the child. It has profound implications of the therapy situation. (This aggressive dialogue will be elaborated in more detail in Chapter 5.)

THE INFANT'S RELATIONSHIP
TO THE WORLD

Winnicott once spelled out the stages of the infant's developing interaction with the outside world. It is basic, perhaps too schematic, but, I think, helpful. Winnicott (1957) described three stages:

1. The infant is a "self contained, a live creature, yet surrounded by space" (p. 19). During this time the subjective experience is that the space and the self are, for the most part, one. It is necessary to add, "for the most part," because we know, as has been discussed, that there is some evokable sense of the surround present from the beginning. The space (and its boundaries) at first is in essence the mother's space, and she is the one who knows how to manage it.

2. In the next stage, the infant "moves an elbow, a knee or straightens out a little. The space has been crossed. The infant has surprised the environment" (p. 19). Winnicott is describing the infant who by virtue of maturational progression and trying out movements has "crossed over" the space and has begun to have some sense of its being a shared space. Winnicott describes it as the infant "surprising" the environment.

3. The caretaker reacts to events in the environment as "small" as the doorbell ringing or the kettle boiling over. The baby feels the startled response. "This time," writes Winnicott, "the environment has surprised the infant."

Winnicott implies that if all is well during stage 1, the "stage is set" for stage 2. If the new sorties into the world are received graciously by the mother, the crucial third stage can be navigated by both parties in an optimal manner. If new experiences are not *impingements* to the mother, Winnicott explains that "the infant who has found the world in this way becomes, in time, ready to welcome the surprises that the world has in store." Winnicott feels that if the mother is careful, she can prevent the world (and herself) from impinging too much on the infant "before the infant has found it! By a live and breathing quietness you follow the life in the infant with the life in yourself, and you wait for the gestures that come from the infant, gestures that lead to your being discovered" (p. 20). This poignant passage epitomizes Winnicott's sensitivity to the nuances of this important interaction.

5

Developmental Lines Involving the Self and Its Functions

This chapter is devoted to providing the reader with a beginning sense of what I consider to be one of Winnicott's most important contributions: the developmental lines that involve the self and its functions. This requires looking at the relationship of the self to itself and to the object world. The latter will be discussed in the next chapter.

First, however, it is necessary to clarify just what is a Winnicottian self. A Winnicottian self is not a clear category. In a paper on countertransference (Winnicott 1960a), as he began discussing the artificiality or authenticity of psychoanalytic language, Winnicott gratuitously gave us this statement: "A word like 'self' naturally knows more than we do; it uses us and can command us" (see Schacht 1988). Was Winnicott this anthropomorphic and theoretically nihilistic? I don't think so, as he wrote of many aspects of the self: its origins, its development, and its possible fates. As Schacht (1988) has stressed, Winnicott's self was involved in experiencing and in the continuous process of its own evolution. Winnicott realized how difficult it is to translate such a crucial concept into mere words, how providing too much closure on the term might stop the developmental process of theory building both in himself and his followers. Thus, another of his legacies is that of providing us with an opportunity to work with an essential concept that is perched between the poles of definition and nondefinition. When Kohut was working out the ideas that led to the establishment of his self psychology, he took a similar attitude toward prematurely closing off a definition of the self.

Before I begin to spell out more specifically the Winnicottian developmental lines (some of which were quite explicit in his work, others more implicit and needing to be partially inferred), it is important to place Winnicott in a more detailed temporal and conceptual perspective with the contemporary psychoanalytically informed researchers of infants. Winnicott, like so many analysts of his day, fashioned himself a researcher. He was serious about his careful observation and notation of infant and child behavior and of the analyses of adults. He called his analyses of borderline and psychotic patients "research analyses," reflecting his belief that an analysis could be considered research, as well as his own concern about the apostasy involved in analyzing the unanalyzable (i.e., if they were research cases, then the heresy was canceled out). But in Winnicott's day, psychoanalysis had not become solidly involved in infant research and instead was dependent on reconstructions from adult anaysis and anecdotal accounts concerning children. Just think of how much mileage Freud's fascinating and important observations of his nephew playing with a string and spool have achieved.

In Winnicott's and Mahler's and Hartmann's day, the prevailing psychoanalytic creation of myth was that of an "in the beginning" undifferentiated state, out of which emerged the ego and its functions, consciousness, self-consciousness, differentiation, and gradually developing separation. Winnicott emphasized the mother's role from day one (witness his stage of primary maternal preoccupation, where for a matter of weeks the mother is almost totally devoted to the infant). However, it would be granting him too much credit to say that he fully recognized the very early built-in capacities to differentiate self from others and one object from another. For the first weeks of life, he tended to use terms such as *merger, ego relatedness,* and the phase of *holding.* He described this time as one of rather optimal attunement between mother and child, in order to contrast it with the necessity for the combined maturational and maternal facilitating factors for ushering the infant into a stage of gradual disillusionment that would ultimately lead to the internalization of externally satisfied needs and the capacity for self regulation. It should be granted that to his credit Winnicott saw the crucial very early importance of the maturational processes and their interaction with maternal attunement.

I want to place Winnicott's view of his early unintegrated state of the infant and his concept of subsequent development in the context of the recent contributions of the psychoanalytic child observers and researchers. The current view from some of the latter is that there are wired-in capacities for differentiation and separation and that there are no clear-cut phases of development. Development continues in complex overlapping ways, and so-called stages of advance can occur simultaneously. Some of this was hinted at by such important developmentalists as Mahler and Winnicott, but it was never organized into a new life-span concept that supersedes the stage approach built into psychoanalysis, beginning, of course, with the classical stages of libidinal development (Freud 1905). In addition, there tends to be a contemporary view of the self as constituted within a sensitive intersubjective milieu that is continuously interacting with progressive developmental flow, all occurring more in a spiral, or more aptly, helix, rather than a straight line model. Emde (1983) stresses the seeming "paradoxical truth of self that our heritage guarantees both our species-wide commonness and our individual uniqueness." This is a quote from his excellent summary of recent conceptual and experimental findings in a paper entitled "The Prerepresentational Self and Its Affective Core."

Emde stresses our affective core as the basic means of under-standing others, and yet he gives strong emphasis to the intersub-jective process as the mode through which the affective core of the prerepresentational self is expressed. He is concerned with self regulation and its development and demonstrates his work on the power of social referencing (the infant's observations of maternal facial expressions and how they affect performance of a given task, in this case, negotiating a visual cliff). Emde stresses his view of the self as a *process* and not "as a psychic structure which is simply acquired at age 1 1/2."

What is a bit surprising is that in Emde's almost six packed pages of bibliography, Winnicott is not mentioned. It is surprising, since Winnicott was so involved in the prerepresentational, preverbal areas: he tried to show that the paradoxes of development were merely two sides of an integrated process; he continuously stressed the interaction of psyche and soma and the self and the other; and he was more concerned with affective and experiential factors than he was with drive or structural factors. I suspect Emde's omission was an oversight. But the fact that Winnicott worked in a different era and in a different manner should also be taken into account. Winnicott did not shy from the poetic as a source of knowing and of communicating. After all, the creative processes were at the core of his interests. In a fascinating paper, "Wordsworth and Winnicott in the Area of Play," John Turner (1988) describes the important similarities in the thinking and style of Winnicott and Wordsworth (Winnicott had read and quoted Wordsworth). Turner reminds us of a well-known quote from the poet's preface to *Lyrical Ballads*: "Poetry is the breath and finer spirit of all knowledge; it is the impassioned expression which is in the countenance of all Science." Winnicott worked on the personal, clinical, and sometimes poetic level and tried to be as rigorous and scientific as he could. Adam Phillips (1988), the author of *Winnicott*, one of Frank Kermode's Modern Masters series, put it in his own way: "It is also fair to recognize that Winnicott had the psychoanalytic virtues of his scientific vices: he did not become systematically coherent at the cost of his own inventiveness" (p. 99).

In spite of the fact that Winnicott did get a lot of it right (although not all of it), he used broad observational and clinical methods in arriving at his, at the time, startling conclusions. And then he reported his work in a series of overlapping papers that were never organized into a true book, but rather into loosely integrated collections of papers. And his style ran anywhere from the standard psychoanalytic to the conversational to the poetic. I think these factors tended to discourage some of our more modern and rigorous developmental researchers from acknowledging him as one of their forefathers. Stern (1985), in his near revolutionary *The Interpersonal World of the Infant,* did discuss Winnicott a number of times, but perhaps the clinical side to his book must have been a basis for his attraction to Winnicott.

My guess would be that the process, life-span view of the development of the self would have been most congenial to Winnicott. I am sure he would have applauded the ingenious experiments that are being conducted on little infants. Much of the general system way of seeing the personality is built into his work. What he offers us is the wisdom of a master clinician who watched what he did in true psychoanalytic and scientific fashion. It is in the extrapolation of new ideas about infant development to the treatment of the older child and the adult that he showed his genius, and in which he has so much to offer to us.

THE DEVELOPMENT OF THE SUBJECTIVE
AND THE OBJECTIVE SELF

Winnicott wrote about the formation of the basic self mainly from two standpoints: as part of his general theory of development and within discussions of his concept of the true and the false self. One of the best places to find the first is in his paper "From Dependence towards Independence in the Development of the Individual"

(1963c), where he spells out three stages of the "journey from dependence to independence." He makes it clear from the start that this journey involves the personal, the contingencies of the environment, and their interaction. He writes, "Health means both health of the individual and health of society, and full maturity of the individual is not possible in an immature or ill social setting" (p. 84). Here Winnicott declares himself in the tradition of social psychologists Mead and Cooley, but with the all-important difference that he is taking constitutional givens and the reality of personality into account. Having plusses on one side of the equation tends to compensate for minuses on the other. For him the crux is the intermediate area where inner and outer interact.

Winnicott divides his journey into three stages: (1) Absolute dependence, (2) Relative dependence, and (3) Towards independence. Essentially he sees the stage of absolute dependence as one in which "at the beginning the infant is entirely dependent on the physical provision of the live mother and her womb or her infant care" (p. 84). But Winnicott doesn't leave it at that. He points to the paradox (in a manner reminiscent of Emde) that the infant is "at one and the same time dependent and independent." On the other hand, "the parents are dependent on the infant's inherited tendencies" (p. 85). By these he includes "all that is inherited, including the maturational processes, and perhaps the pathological inherited trends, and these have a reality of their own, and no one can alter these" (p. 84).

Essentially, the parents have the opportunity to accept these givens and attempt to attune themselves to them. But Winnicott cautions, "But the environment does not make the child. At best it enables the child to realize potential" (p. 85). At the earliest times of biological dependency the mother's main job is to attune herself to these biological and potential or incipient psychological needs. Winnicott stresses the bio-psychological nature of the infant's needs and the mother's phase of primary maternal preoccupation, where "the mother is preoccupied with (or better, 'given over to') the care of her baby, which at first seems like a part of herself; moreover she is very much identified with the baby and knows quite well what the baby is feeling like" (p. 85). The time is quite analagous to Mahler's symbiotic phase. The work of Stern and others now sees the dependence–independence process beginning from day one. This means that the optimal, virtually perfect attunement that the concept of total dependence involves is not necessary. Winnicott would not have much trouble with this modification, since he saw the world relativistically, more in terms of *degrees* of "good enough" rather than perfection phasing into good enough.

The more the mother is there when the infant needs her to be, the more a sense of continuity, a "going-on-being," a core identity that is far from consciousness is laid down. Winnicott speaks of the mother's holding and securing functions being able to protect the baby from impingements, or at least to keep them to a minimum. "Any impingement, or failure of adaptation, causes a reaction in the infant, and the reaction breaks up the going-on-being. If reacting to impingements is the pattern of an infant's life, then there is a serious interference with the natural tendency that exists in the infant to become an integrated unit, able to continue to have a self with a past, present, and future" (p. 86). Winnicott speaks of this process, when optimal, as laying down the "keel" of future mental health.

Moving a bit up the developmental timetable (in Winnicott's terms), we can begin to speak of a primitive psyche, contributed to by the mother's empathic ability to meet the dawning psychological needs of the infant just as they are experienced, leading to the illusion that the breast, or the bottle, or the "hold" were created by the infant. The nascent, but still presumably unconscious, sense of being able to create something, to make something happen, and its ultimate corollary, to exist in the world, is beginning to develop. Winnicott stresses the sequence of *being* and then *doing*. They are not stages but rather different facets of the process of forming the prerepresentational self. They can occur in alternating sequences as well as simultaneously.

Winnicott's ideas on mirroring (1971b) are quite important here. When the caretaker is empathically tuned, there can be a visceral imitation of the infant's facial expression, bodily stance, movement patterns, babblings, and other sounds. The infant looks and feels into this human mirror and sees himself or herself. On some level, it must feel good. And you can change the output and "make" the mirror feed back the change, thus having an impact on the world. In ways such as this, the sense of self develops. To the degree that this self is a visceral, id-like, sensorimotor self, it has the components of what Winnicott calls the true self.

The more objective self and the beginning sense of separateness occur when the mother's adaptation to the infant's needs begins to show flaws. The moment of need is not always met. And the mirror feeds back a creature that has but little self-ness in it. The infant is discovering the world, and itself. It is here that the *necessity* for good enough mothering comes in, for too much merging and identification impedes the formation of a healthy self that is neither merely reflecting others nor being dominated by them. An alteration of self and nonself experiences is required, the whole process occurring in an empathic, basically supporting, and reasonably consistent facilitating environment.

The boundaries of the self are created in a number of ways. Winnicott stresses, along with the just mentioned processes, the importance of aggressive affects (Winnicott 1971e). By aggressing against an object, the infant places it outside the area of fantasy and omnipotence. The "hurt" object behaves in its own manner; it has to be contended with. If it "holds" and isn't destroyed (by becoming enraged and out of control—dying isn't necessary), the developing infant begins to see it existing in its own right. A line between the inner and the outer becomes more and more definite. This "line" (which actually is more of a fluctuating membrane that hardens or softens depending on the circumstances that require adaptation) is given more basic stability by interactive play, physical and verbal, and by interactions with transitional objects at the surface of the body (Lorenzer and Orban 1978).

Winnicott is stressing attachment and interpersonal needs, affects, and interactions. In a modern way, ultimately he sees drives as coming into existence *after* primitive affects. Drives, even though they are part of a person, are outside the psyche until they are integrated into it. An unintegrated drive is experienced by the young self as an impingement as much as an outer, unempathic response would be. Presumably, a reasonably stable self can tolerate and integrate burgeoning drives while at the same time it develops defensive ways of handling external impingements.

One of the greatest problems negotiating the Winnicottian canon is his sometimes inconsistent use of the terms *ego* and *self*. This is clearly evident when he talks of his concept of personalization, a linkage of the personality of the growing infant to its somatic existence. He speaks of depersonalization as a "loss of the union between ego and body" (Winnicott 1962, p. 59). Winnicott is referring more to the psychosomatic self in child development. If he had been more accurate in this section of the paper "Ego Integration in Child Development," he would have used the term *ego* only when he saw it with reference to the id, as they are both on the same level of conceptualization (Freud 1923). Needless to say, Winnicott saw the ability of the caretaker to interact with the child's "gut" self and help to create a psyche–soma union as an important component of the healthy self.

Winnicott calls his third aspect of development "towards independence," implying that it is never an absolute goal, but that the relative amounts of dependence and independence are gradually balanced on the side of the latter. This fluid concept is almost identical in its nature to Mahler's last subphase of her separation–individuation process, which she designates as on the way to self- and object-constancy (Mahler et al. 1975).

THE DEVELOPMENT OF SELF-CONSTANCY

Within an object relations universe, it is not possible to separate self-constancy from object-constancy. Inter-subjective interactions, that is, interactions between attuned subjects and objects, lead to the disillusionments stressed in the systems of both Winnicott and Kohut. The infant's or toddler's reactive aggression and/or depression lead to graduated internalizations so that the experience of affective memory of the self or object can be self-evoked (Fraiberg 1969).

Winnicott's loose usage of terminology as he struggled to find his own language and milieu creates problems for the reader in the area of internalized constancy. His original concept of self is a broad one that has to do with the environmental world and the necessity of establishing a limiting membrane between the two. But the outside here is the environment-mother, not the object-relating, introjective, or potential whole mother. When development has progressed to allow the sense of an integrated rather than part object self and mother, then we can speak of the representational world. It is here that Winnicott finds it necessary to retain the concept of an ego, a place where self and object representations can reside.

I think that once the representational world has been established and we can begin to speak of whole objects and symbolic forms, the Winnicottian psyche has to be looked at at different conceptual levels. One of these is the broad issue of the interactive relationship of the self with others, either other human beings or the anthropomorphized nonhuman environment. Some of the latter can be subsumed under sophisticated, more abstracted versions of transitional objects and phenomena (see Chapter 7). A second conceptual level would see the introjective world interacting with the extrajective, "real" world in a manner similar to the transitional process occurring between the broader self and the outside world.

The terms *self-constancy* and *object-constancy* are well ensconced in the literature, particularly in so far as the literature has revolved around Mahler's having chosen them for her fourth subphase. In a recent paper (Grolnick 1987), a more Winnicottian terminology for self- and object-constancy was proposed. Winnicott's and Mahler's views of the establishment of inner constancy and relative independence from the need for external stimuli are quite similar. By designating this important phase as being on the way to merely potential, nonachievable constancy, and by the very nature of the term *constancy,* the essential interactive, feedback state between internalized and externalized forms that we consider to be present in healthy individuals is not given its just due. The admittedly awkward term *transitional process stability* might be preferable, for it is a *process* that is internalized, not constant structures. For the sake of argument, if we took self- and object-constancy to their reductio ad absurdum, there would not be a *healthy* dependency on others, nor the capacity to move in a dependent position during emotional need or physical illness. While Mahler and her co-workers clearly would recognize this, their terminology for the fourth subphase does not take this recognition into account. Psychoanalysis has not infrequently tended to inadvertently imply certain goals that are impossible to attain, and the actual attainment of those goals would not necessarily be desirable. Included would be genital primacy, ego autonomy, and now, self- and object-constancy. Again, no doubt the theoreticians would have readily acknowledged that they were only designating ideal states. However, to the degree that language structures the way we think about the world (including psychoanalytic theories), a terminology that reflects the crucial importance of optimal *degrees* of internalization and advance and the lifelong interplay between earlier and later modes seems not to be in order. The terms *self-* and *object-constancy,* with their heuristic and now historical strength, are here to stay for some time. But there is a need to reexamine self- and object-constancy and Winnicott's less well-known third stage of "towards independence." That Winnicott actually had a more process view of so-called independence is made clear in his important paper "The Capacity to Be Alone" (Winnicott 1958).

A few more words on self-constancy, or the self aspects of transitional process stability, are in order. There is a built-in maturational core of self that, if recognized, reflected back, and validated can lead to sense of, and the reality of, a continuity of the self. To the degree that there are self and object stability in the caretaker, the capacity for that caretaker, early on, to serve as a mirror echoing back—in all sensory modalities—images of the alive self can be taken for granted as serving as a facilitator of the maturational core of the self. If, however, the caretaker sees the infant as part of a split world, a good baby one time and a bad baby another, the underlying images of a good enough, human, loved baby will not develop sufficiently to provide a self-evocable stable self system. This involves both the subjective sense of self and the ability of an objective self to retain a consistent identity in spite of the many roles life directs us to play. Certainly we are all aware of people, some of whom are patients, who have managed to develop a core identity that is recognized (objectively) by others, yet these same individuals experience themselves as all things to all people, or chameleons, as fly-by-nights, or as only episodically solid. How the objective self and the subjective self develop separately is no doubt due to many factors, including the simultaneous presence of strong constitutional givens and a lack of a corresponding facilitating partner. How it happens can be studied in our patients and deserves careful research, as this is a common affliction.

THE DEVELOPMENT OF A SENSE OF SECURITY AND SELF-CONTROL

This developmental line cannot be separated from the one involving self-stability. Feeling a reliability of self processes contributes greatly to feeling secure. Winnicott writes in a chapter entitled "On Security" (1960c): "There must build up inside each child a belief in something, not only something that is good but also something that is reliable and durable, or that recovers after having been hurt or allowed to perish" (pp. 30–31). Winnicott goes on to stress the capacity of parents to protect their offspring from the impingements and traumas that occur from the environment and from the drives, or impulses.

Then Winnicott proceeds in his characteristic manner to use another sense of the word *security,* reminding us of "stone walls and iron bars." The reader thinks of maximum security prisons and the like. Here Winnicott indicates that there are early times when feeling protected and controlled is very much related to feeling secure. This is at a time when there has not been sufficient internalization of external control into self-control.

Then Winnicott, using his concept of the importance of developmental aggression (not drive-tinged sadism), shows that part of the process of being able to feel secure is to test the security system around you. This is most clear in the adolescent. He writes:

> They carry with them a sense of security and this is constantly being reinforced by their tests of their parents and family, of their schoolteachers and friends, and of all sorts of people they meet. Having found the locks and bolts securely fastened, they proceed to unlock them and to break them open; they burst out. And again and again they burst out. [p. 32]

Winnicott then asks, "Why do adolescents especially make such tests?" He answers, "It seems to be mainly because they are meeting frighteningly new and strong feelings in themselves, and they wish to know that the external controls are still there. But at the same time they must prove that they can break through these controls and establish themselves as themselves" (p. 32). He deplores external, mechanical controls, but advocates controls coming from a "living relationship," a dialogue between the adolescent and his potentially controlling figures. Winnicott then tops off the paper with the analogy of the artist who for him- or herself, and ourselves, is continuously involved in a struggle between inner impulses and the sense of security. He sees this as a lifelong dialectic. Winnicott ends the paper with, "So I see it this way: good conditions in the early stages lead to a sense of security, and a sense of security leads on to self-control, and when self-control is a fact, then security that is imposed is an insult" (p. 33). It is unnecessary to add anything more.

THE DEVELOPMENT OF SELF-ASSERTIVENESS

While self-assertiveness is not a specific developmental line that Winnicott spelled out, it is implied throughout his work. It is worth teasing out since the origins of this capacity and a history of failure in its good enough development have important clinical significance.

First, a clarification is needed. Psychoanalysis has always distinguished between aggression, which tended to be originally associated with the aggressive drive (and later with aggressive affects as well), and assertiveness. The latter was considered to be a healthy ego capacity that could be involved in conflict, particularly when the aggressive drives were involved. Somewhat in contrast, Winnicott tended to regard aggression in a healthier developmental sense, referred to the "positive values of destructiveness" (Winnicott 1971e, p. 94), often used it more in its affective rather than drive form, and did not find it necessary to make the distinction between aggression and assertiveness. It is implied, however.

Winnicott saw aggression as one of the necessary parts of the process of the infant's ability to place the object outside the projective world and into the sphere of reality. If the object can be attacked and destroyed again and again, and survive just as often, the infant develops a sense that there is an outside that has the origins of stability. This process leads to what Winnicott terms the *use of the object*. In his paper "The Use of an Object and Relating through Identifications" (1971e), he states, "By 'use' I do not mean 'exploitation.' " But he also stresses the difference between object-relating as a developmental achievement and the use of the object. He writes:

> Object-relating is an experience of the subject that can be described in terms of the subject as an isolate. When I speak of the use of an object, however, I take object-relating for granted, and add new features that involve the nature and the behavior of the object. For instance, the object, if it is to be used, must necessarily be real in the sense of being part of shared reality, not a bundle of projections. [p. 88]

Winnicott recognized in this that a simple relationship with another person is not enough. One of the dimensions of a relationship that had not been stressed previously is just this ability of each partner to utilize the other, based on a reasonably clear perception of the other and his or her strengths and vulnerabilities. I would venture to say that this use of the object overlaps with what has been termed *assertiveness* in the psychoanalytic literature.

In effect, Winnicott told us that to be an assertive individual, one must first feel that an effective self exists; one must feel real through the loving interplay of a relationship; one must create a sphere of outer reality by aggressing against the object and being reassured that it still exists; and one has to be able to not only relate to but use the partner who, in turn, will or should use you. In a broad sense, virtually every aspect of Winnicott's version of the development of the self is involved in creating an individual who feels a sense of being able to impact the world, and hence able to be assertive with and know how to use that world.

The therapeutic implications here are fairly self-evident. If the patient has not had the environmental facilitation for the capacity to be assertive, a therapeutic development field must be built. After enough trust is established (often hard-won trust), a milieu must be created that enables the patient to, at first hesitantly but more and more firmly, aggress against and "destroy" the real therapist. This is not too likely to be happening when the patient aggresses against the transferential therapist, the symbolic therapist and what he or she stands for. It is aggression against the *real person* of the therapist, including personality traits and flaws and real empathic failures and errors, that counts. I think this is consistent with Winnicott's stress on the developmental ability to ultimately interact with the object outside of the projective (and I would add here, displaced) world. Too often patients and therapists deal with a kind of make-believe aggression that does not have the barbs of steel sufficient to hurt or "destroy" the therapist. Perhaps one of the best tests of this is whether or not the patient's attack does get to the therapist. If it doesn't, you may have to try again!

THE DEVELOPMENT OF A SENSE
OF AUTHENTICITY

Winnicott was dedicated to authenticity, naturalness, spontaneity, and freedom within responsibility. It characterized his life, his works, and his letters (Rodman 1987). Nowhere in his work was this dedication so well demonstrated and so successful as in his concept of the true and false self (Winnicott 1960b). Here he took an idea that had gained the interest of philosophers, existentialists, psychologists, and psychoanalysts such as Jung. However, Winnicott showed the concept not as a dichotomy but as a spectrum and a hierarchy. And he traced its developmental origins in a way that had not been done previously.

Winnicott's true self is partly a given and partly requires a validation. Winnicott presumes a primal authenticity and innocence. The infant is born with sensorimotor and sensoritonic reactions to its own body and to outside ministrations. Winnicott sees the core of the personality as being laid down prior to the formation of drives, although ultimately drive experiences are involved. What does this mean? In keeping with studies on constitutional differences, Winnicott sees each infant as a unique orchestra that produces its own melodies with its own rhythmic and tonal variations. If the caretaker has a reasonably good ear, the infant's music can be heard and responded to with care and empathy. The orchestra sets the tone for a while. Winnicott stresses the spontaneous gesture and, later, the personal idea that hopefully can be recognized and met. This process was spelled out by him in detail in his paper on mirroring (1971b) where, using various sensory modalities (not only the visual), the mother reflects back what she sees and feels. We all know how good it feels when another person can feed back something to ourselves that is highly personal. It must be something like that. This authentication and validation must occur in a myriad of ways in order for a certain amount of cacophony to appear on the scene and be received in a healthy developmental manner. After a while, the attunement and mistuning appear simultaneously as well as consecutively.

It is at this point that the false self makes its appearance. Winnicott makes it clear that when the infant feels solid enough it is ready for mother-made rather than baby-inspired perceptions. Some of this is imitated and subjected to the process of Piagetian accommodation. As with Piaget, accommodation and assimilation are in an interactive equilibrium. Without a false self, or in healthy terms, a social self, a true self would never be able to survive in the world. This is nothing so startling: Winnicott merely organized the concept in a helpful way. It is the times when the caretaker's mistiming and mistuning broadcast *too much* of the other and not enough of the baby that a pathological false self can occur. Here the unfortunate child, and ultimately adult, feels more like the other than his- or herself. The sense of inauthenticity or of being a phony takes over. Of course there has to be enough true self formation in order to have a sense of falseness. But the situation can be so severe that the true self is completely buried and protected by the false self so that the falseness is noticed only by others—these people are usually considered to be severe "as-if" personalities. If pathological false self formation is too severe, then the personality becomes too accommodative, too compliant, and, by definition, loses too much of the creative spontaneity and innovativeness that are associated with the true self and its origins.

Winnicott's all-pervading interest in the formation of the self and its vicissitudes continued on, resulting in one of his most complex papers, "Communicating and Not Communicating Leading to a Study of Certain Opposites" (Winnicott 1963a), three years after his true and false self paper. This paper (Winnicott 1963a) may have been a response to potential abuses of the true and false self concept. Winnicott wrote in the second paragraph of this paper, which was initially delivered in San Francisco:

> Starting from no fixed place I soon came, while preparing this paper for a foreign society, to staking a claim, to my surprise, to the right not to communicate. This was a protest from the core of me to the frightening fantasy of being infinitely exploited. In another language this would be the fantasy of being eaten or swallowed up. In the language of this paper it is the *fantasy of being found.* [p. 179]

By presenting a true self that is so alive and creative, in 1960 Winnicott had implicitly asked his therapist–readers to help in the crusade of discovering and unearthing that true self, much in the spirit that the early id psychoanalysts had with respect to the id and the primary process. While it was implied in his 1960 paper (1960a), Winnicott now spells this out quite explicitly: "At the center of each person is an incommunicado element, and this is sacred and most worthy of preservation" (p. 187). He went on to warn against the danger that psychoanalysis (presumably both Winnicottian and classical) could inadvertently violate this sacredness. He wrote, "We can understand the hatred people have of psycho-analysis which has penetrated a long way into the human personality, and which provides a threat to the human individual in his need to be secretly isolated. The question is: how to be isolated without having to be insulated?" (p. 187).

Winnicott's answer essentially sees optimal nonthreatening communication taking place through the medium of his intermediate transitional dialogue "that slides out of playing into cultural experience of every kind" (p. 188). He contrasts this form of communication with the polarities, communication that is *forever silent* and communication that is *explicit,* indirect, and pleasurable. He is also concerned with the therapist being fooled by someone who is simply not communicating but who may be only resting, as contrasted with the patient who is trying to communicate an *inability* to communicate. Winnicott is concerned with a patient's "negation of silence or negation of an active or reactive non-communicating" (p. 188). When a schizoid patient covers up or negates his or her basic state of noncommunication, it is possible for an analysis "to become an infinitely prolonged collusion of the analyst with the patient's negation of non-communication" (p. 180). The false outer communication can be misread by the therapist as authentic and the treatment proceed without going anywhere. Winnicott advises that in this kind of situation, things can be turned around if the patient can be silent and if the therapist can learn to wait.

Winnicott also warns us of an even more dangerous state of affairs in the same kind of patient where the central self is secreted away, when the therapist may just reach inside to the deepest layers. In this case, the therapeutic activity has actually reached its target. The danger here in the schizoid patient is that the therapist assumes inordinate powers. The treatment should have been put on hold until the patient was given a chance to creatively discover him- or herself. Sometimes it is better to be lost for a while before being found.

Winnicott traced out a developmental line of the self that involved a dialectical process between the social and the true self. It was another version of his focus on the interplay between what appears to be polarities, but ultimately turns out to be facets of a complex, developmental process. By absorbing what Winnicott had to say about the quality of authenticity and the developmental lines that help to create it, a therapist can have a good start learning how to offer the patient an ebb and flow of empathy, dissonance, and daring mixed with the ability to hold back and wait.

THE DEVELOPMENT OF SELF-POSSESSION

Self-possession is a quality that Winnicott did not write about in any extended manner, although he did comment on ownership and possession. The self-possessed person feels a sense of continuity and of self-reliability. Winnicott reiterated how important caretaker holding, handling, securing, and controlling are for a self that has a sense of stability that extends from the past through the present into the future. Much of this is built into Winnicott's view of the basic, true self. The following paragraph from his paper "Communication between Infant and Mother, and Mother and Infant, Compared and Contrasted" (1968) is typical:

> The mother's capacity to meet the changing and developing needs of this one baby enables this one baby to have a line of life, relatively unbroken; and enables this baby to experience both unintegrated or related states in confidence in the holding that is actual, along with oft-repeated phases of the integration that is part of the baby's inherited growth tendency. The baby goes easily to and fro from integration to the ease of relaxed unintegration and the accumulation of these experiences becomes a pattern, and forms a basis for what the baby expects. The baby comes to believe in a reliability in the inward processes leading to integration into a unit. [p. 97]

A person who is self-possessed seems steady, able to stand on his or her feet, and not in danger of falling. Here it is necessary to return to another of Winnicott's concepts. He includes the fear of "falling forever" (1962) as one of the primitive unthinkable psychotic-level anxieties. One of the places this early terror is discussed is his interesting paper, "Fear of Breakdown" (1974). He lists the primitive agonies ("anxiety is not a strong enough word here") and their defenses. The defense for the terror of falling forever is "self-holding." He had defined this previously in his ego integration paper (1962) as "self-holding, or the development of a caretaker self and the organization of an aspect of the personality that is false (false in that what is showing is a derivative not of the individual but of the mothering aspects of the infant–mother coupling)." Thus Winnicott brings in a new level of this developmental line. Optimally the mother's caretaking and holding activities gradually become internalized into the healthy aspects of false (or social) self formation. Presumably the healthy infant feels both a sense of the basic reliability of the true self and the later developed internalized reliability of the other. I think that the graduated internalization of these precursors can lead to an important aspect of the quality of self-possession.

Another way of studying self-possession is through primary creativity and the concept of the transitional process. By allowing the infant to have the illusion that the caretaker's response was under its own control, primary creativity provides the infant with a very early sense of making something happen, of creating either an object or a response. Soon transitional objects and or transitional phenomena appear in this intermediate area and become the infant's first treasured possessions. The mother cannot be owned, by definition. But the illusion of pure blissful ownership can be sustained with reference to the passive transitional object. Of course, as has been described earlier, transitional objects and phenomena are only the first steps toward the development of, hopefully, an equally treasured symbolic and cultural world. When the experiences of primary creativity and the development of transitional objects and phenomena and the symbolic world have proceeded in a good enough manner and have gradually become internalized, the individual can feel a deep sense of owning, yes, possessing, internally what was once possessed only within the realm of illusion. I am referring here to the sense of being in possession of and in control of one's own self and mind.

An additional factor here is Winnicott's way of looking at the formation of the psychosomatic self (1949). If the caretaker can react empathically to bodily actions and rhythms and help endow our early primitive symbols with a body and a texture, the sense of owning the self can include the body. The adult quality of self-possession has a definite bodily component. The self-possessed person is in control of and composed in mind *and* manner. He or she looks self-possessed without having to utter a word. When he or she does speak, the impression is reinforced.

Adult self-possession involves so much more than it does in the toddler, the child, and even the adolescent. I am emphasizing that it involves a developmental line that Winnicott implied throughout his work. If a therapist can take into account the issues of holding, primary creativity, and the transitional process aspects of the therapeutic interaction with the patient, I believe it is possible to contribute to building more self-possessiveness in patients who have had difficulty in this line of development.

THE DEVELOPMENT OF THE CAPACITY
TO BE ALONE

Perhaps Winnicott's (1958) paper "The Capacity to Be Alone" is one of his most important, in that it intersects with most of his basic concepts. Again, a careful reading of the paper provides the best way to learn about and have a feeling for a developmental line that is as vastly important in early life as it is in virtually any clinical or life situation. Winnicott begins his now classic paper, "I wish to make an examination of the capacity of the individual to be alone, acting on the assumption that this capacity is one of the most important signs of maturity in emotional development" (p. 29). Winnicott then goes on to stress the paradox involved in his concept, that being alone is at the same time being in the presence of someone else. The rub is that he is referring to a developmental line, so that the child who is at first able to play and explore alone with his caretaker present but in the background, given healthy development, eventually becomes the individual who has internalized that present but not interfering caretaker into a self-evocative function. Thus, the mature adult is able to tolerate extended periods of being able to work, play, and be productive while alone because there has been someone there, now inside, who is watching over things and providing the sense of not being lonely during activity. Of course, as has been stressed previously (see the section on self-constancy in this chapter), internalization and externalization are always in some equilibrium. The healthy individual eventually would become lonely, the presence of the other (hopefully) not being internalized enough to provide an *everlasting* presence. Ultimately, most of us need real play- and workmates to provide an optimal internalization–externalization balance.

It is significant that Winnicott has given us a gradually developing and internalizing growth pattern, but at the same time a model for many aspects of living. In his "Capacity to Be Alone" paper he describes the couple following coitus. "It is perhaps fair to say that after satisfactory intercourse each partner is alone and is contented to be alone. Being able to enjoy being alone along with another person who is also alone is in itself an experience of health" (p. 31). Then it is not hard to use Winnicott's deceptively simple concept in understanding the artist's desire to be alone during the creative process. And, as will be elaborated more later on, the very psychotherapeutic and psychoanalytic situations consist, to some degree, of the patient being alone in the presence of the therapist. If the patient cannot do this, then the therapist must back up and take Winnicott's early developmental line of the capacity to be alone into account with his or her patient.

The concept of the capacity to be alone involves the consideration of the externalized and internalized object as well as the self.

Since self and object are intrinsically related, both developmentally and in actuality, the object world has been very much involved. In a similar manner, the next chapter, which considers developmental lines concerning the object world, will also be concerned with the self.

6

The Development of the Sense of an Object and Object Relatedness

Winnicott has stated, or at least implied, that there is no such thing as an object (without a subject). "But," the reader can ask, "isn't the psychoanalytic school that Winnicott associated himself with called the object relations school?" It is reasonable to say that this school has only half a name and that it could be called the self and object relations school. However, historically it was the emphasis on the object world, the facilitating environment, that distinguished the British middle school. The Kleinian object predominately emphasized the inner object—hence the justification for calling Klein the "mother" of the object relations school. However, it was Winnicott and the others of the middle school who emphasized the reality of the *external object*, how facilitation by the environment created by the real caretaker is necessary for maturation to be primed and interacted with throughout its developmental journey. And certainly it was Winnicott who showed that the environment and the maturational processes were in a continuous feedback system with each other.

The very young infant "creates" the object that is presented by an empathic caretaker, and the result, a subjective object, "lives" within the world of the infant's omnipotence. The subjective object is not yet internalized and is not an introject; if it were, there would already be a corresponding concept of the objective object.

The subjective object "graduates" into the objective object through a combination of "good enough" graded environmental failure and the ability of the infant and child to aggress against the object without destroying it. The developmental maternal "failure" that follows the primary creative subjective object helps to internalize the object and create a "limiting membrane" that serves as the base for reality testing. Then, both subsequently and simultaneously, the aggression against the object helps to place it outside the omnipotent, creative sphere of the infant, giving it a reality of its own and contributing to the infant's ability to use the object. The result of this much more complex process is the gradual (very gradual) birth of the "object objectively perceived," as Winnicott liked to put it. It is important here to recognize that Winnicott was not merely delineating the developmental line of the internalization of previously external objects and their functions. The process needs the *actual* facilitating ability of the caretaker to provide developmentally graded disillusionments and the ability to stand up against the onslaught of infantile aggression without being destroyed, either literally or figuratively. Traditional psychoanalysis took the environmental side for granted and didn't link it intrinsically with the gradually evolving theory of developmental internalization. This does not make Winnicott an environmentalist; perhaps we can call him a totalist, as he filled in a vitally important missing space in psychoanalytic developmental theory.

I have just referred to the subjective object graduating into the objectively perceived object. But a part of every reasonably content college student stays with his or her alma mater throughout life. Alma maters wouldn't survive financially if this weren't so. The subjective object stays in derivative form and helps to form the sense of the continuous self that was delineated in the last chapter.

In a Hegelian (1830) manner, Winnicott felt that previous stages weren't given up but remained potentially revivable or actually functioning alongside later derivatives. The external object's non-impinging presence lives on in internalized form, contributing to the adult mature capacity to be alone. It is obvious in these concepts that *what* is internalized (the qualities of the caretaker and of the manner of ministration and facilitation) is just as crucial as the fact that internalization of an external object has taken place. Winnicott referred to the disappearance of a subjective object due to environmental failures as a catastrophic mental event, leading to a situation where the individual is subject to the "unthinkable anxieties," to psychotic terror, to disorder, or a "basic fault," as Balint termed it.

Winnicott refers to the part object not infrequently, believing along traditional lines that part object relations precede whole object relations. Sometimes he refers to the drive for the object in object relational terms and sometimes, particularly early on when he was still more influenced by Klein, he refers to the zonal object of the drive. During the time when the mother is beginning to be seen as a full person, the transitional object becomes an aide, a kind of extended part object that can be retreated to when relations with the whole mother become conflicted (Metcalf and Spitz 1978). Replenishment, or refueling, in the experience with and evoked by the transitional object can give the strength to move on to further interaction with the actual mother.

The sequence of holding, handling, and object-presenting on the part of the caretaker corresponds with Winnicott's (1962) phases of infant integration, personalization and, lastly, object-relating. While this is an oversimplified schema, it can be helpful heuristically and clinically.

The later stages of Winnicott's developmental line of object differentiation and relating is one of his most important contributions to theory and technique. It can be stated in one sentence, but it is most complex: The vicissitudes of object-relating and object relationships influence the level of affective symbolization and the qualities of the symbolic world that each individual brings along from the earliest years. The first meaningful triangulation of the infant–mother dyad, the transitional object, presumably becomes the ancestor of future affectively bathed, mature symbols that have achieved a reasonable degree of independence from their referents and from the primary (human) object (Werner and Kaplan 1963). In the therapy situation, language functions in intermediate space and has the equivalency of a transitional phenomenon. As such it can serve as a mediating object in the same sense that transitional objects and phenomena do in infancy and childhood, offering the patient who has borderline narcissistic, schizoid, or other characterological difficulties a second chance.

In his important paper "The Antisocial Tendency," Winnicott (1956a) works with another aspect of the relationship to the object: object seeking. In a section entitled "The Original Loss," he goes to the heart of the matter:

> At the basis of the anti-social tendency is a good early experience that has been lost. *Surely, it is an essential feature that the infant has reached to a capacity to perceive that the cause of the disaster lies in an environmental failure.* . . . Antisocial children . . . are constantly pressing for (a) cure by environmental provision (unconsciously, or by unconscious motivation) but are unable to make use of it. [pp. 313–314]

Winnicott goes on to describe these patients as having "a drive that could be called object-seeking." As was elaborated in the last chapter, the antisocial patient senses the possibility of a more reliable environment and will continuously test and retest it for its stable and securing qualities. Winnicott stresses the therapist's (or the institution's) "capacity to stand the aggression, to prevent or repair the destruction, to tolerate the nuisance, to recognize the positive element in the antisocial tendency, to provide and preserve the object that is to be sought and found."

Winnicott maintains that once the object-seeking and the period of testing is over, it is necessary for the child "to experience despair in a relationship, instead of hope alone." I think that this therapeutic sequence has wider application than with patients who have anti-social tendencies. Virtually every patient who has had early envi-ronmental failure must spend a long period in treatment finding out and testing out whether the situation gives the appearance of reliability (therapy by definition gives that appearance) or whether it is truly reliable. Clearly, who the therapist is and what kind of training he or she has had is crucial here. Patients will not allow themselves to enter into a true structural regression until they feel the therapist can provide a holding environment that virtually guarantees that the patient will not be dropped. The structural regression that is involved in an effective Winnicottian treatment differs from the topographic regression (referring to levels of con-sciousness) that is advocated for the healthier patient treated in a classical psychoanalytic situation. The reexperience of the infantile neurosis within the transference and memory is not the same as a patient's capacity to regress to a state of dependency and less internalization in order to reexperience serious early failures within the therapeutic situation. The healthier patient has already internal-ized holding and is able to trust, whereas the patients Winnicott tended to treat required an externalized version of this function that had to be provided by the therapist.

A pivotal Winnicottian concept pertaining to the object is his admittedly artificial division of the early mother into two compo-nents, the "environment-mother" and the "object-mother." While the concept was already present in his 1945 paper "Primitive Emotional Development," it became increasingly important in two 1963 papers, "Communicating and Not Communicating Leading to a Study of Certain Opposites" (1963a) and "The Development of the Capacity for Concern" (1963b). (The latter will be discussed more fully in the next section.) Winnicott's introduction to the subject in his "On Communication" paper is a little confusing and deserves clarification. He writes, "The infant develops two kinds of relation-ships at one and the same time—that to the environment-mother and that to the object, which becomes the object-mother. The environment-mother is human, and the object-mother is a thing, although it is also the mother or part of her."

Winnicott makes it clear that both of these maternal functions go on *simultaneously* during a given period in the infant's life. Winni-cott means that the "human" environment-mother is one way of looking at the principal caretaker's ability to provide a reliable, consistent, good enough empathic situation for the infant to have and fall back on if necessary. Winnicott speaks of the shattering effect of an infant discovering, unconsciously for the most part, that the environment-mother is really unreliable.

In contrast to the environment-mother, the object-mother is the more traditional psychoanalytic mother—she is the object of the infant's libidinal and aggressive drives. At an early point when drives are raw and sadism is in the air, the mother can be attacked "ruthlessly," as Winnicott liked to say it. The object-mother must be conflictual and require defensive operations in contrast to the environment-mother, who provides a supportive, steady backdrop of holding and care. Winnicott goes on to elaborate in his paper on concern: "The object-mother has to be found to survive the instinct-driven episodes, which have not acquired the full force of fantasies of oral sadism and other results of fusion" (p. 76). This ruthless little infant has all the Kleinian attributes: "It is not only that the baby imagines that he eats the object, but also that the baby wants to take possession of the contents of the object. If the object is destroyed, it is because of its own survival capacity, not because of the baby's protection of the object" (p. 76). These quotes show how much Winnicott was influenced by Klein even in the early 1960s. In these papers there is a traditional concept of libidinal and aggressive drives alongside Winnicott's object relational position as exempli-fied by his concept of the environment-mother. Later on in the decade, and in many places, affects and drives are sometimes used interchangeably. Also, Winnicott did try to downplay the role of the aggressive drive by substituting "motility" and "destructiveness." In *Playing and Reality* (1971c) he returned to the commonly described "male element or drive aspect of object-relating" and the neglected non-drive female element of "subject-object identity," the "basis of the capacity to be" (p. 81).

I think the use of the drive concept helps to explain why Winnicott calls the object-mother "a thing, although it is also the mother or part of her." The drive object is an erotic zonal concept, that is, oral, anal, and so on; in this sense, traditionally conceptualized drives are directed to *parts* of the mother, not the mother as a whole. Thus the object-mother is not human insofar as the drives are concerned.

THE DEVELOPMENT OF THE CAPACITY
FOR CONCERN

As alluded to above, Winnicott describes an early time when drives still have their primitive qualities, which he called the stage of pre-ruth, or ruthlessness. This oral sadistic onslaught is dealt with, one way or another, by the object-mother, in the setting of a hopefully consistent environment-mother. For Winnicott, the normal course of development comprises a "coming-together in the infant's mind of the object-mother and the environment-mother" (1963b, p. 76). This implies both the preexisting capacity on the infant's part for integration and the presence of an analogous integrative ability on the mother's part, so that her object-functioning is not dissociated from her environmental functioning.

The result of this coming-together in healthy development is that the mother is seen more and more as a whole, real person. The infant develops the sense that there can be a reciprocal giving relationship, an opportunity on the infant's part for what he calls "contributing-in." This also involves an early sense of the capacity to make reparations. Here Winnicott directly borrows a Kleinian concept. However, he is not referring to the affect of guilt, as does Klein in the first part of the first year. Winnicott is describing a preguilt, preoedipal time and is still concerned with dyadic relationships, not the triadic relationships that are involved in the Oedipus complex and its internalization into the superego. By concern, Winnicott means that

> the infant is now becoming able to be concerned, to take responsibility for his or her own instinctual impulses and the functions that belong to them. This provides one of the fundamental constructive elements of play and work. But in the developmental process, it was the opportunity to contribute that enabled concern to be within the child's capacity. [p. 77]

Winnicott is describing what could be called a precursor of the superego and of morality. (This issue will be discussed in the next section.)

Winnicott refers to the kind of situation where the capacity for concern does not develop adequately: "Briefly, failure of the object-mother to survive or of the environment-mother to provide reliable opportunity for reparation leads to a loss of the capacity for concern, and to its replacement by crude anxieties and by crude defenses such as splitting, or disintegration" (p. 78).

Winnicott's concept of concern as a developmental line can be helpful clinically. In his paper on concern, he gives three pertinent clinical examples. His view of concern directly ties in with his "use of the object" concept. A good Winnicottian therapist has to be ready to be "destroyed." What is being added here is the importance of the down-but-not-out therapist being able to acknowledge the patient's nascent and eventually more full-blown constructive and reparative actions, even though these may not be directed at the therapist, as they can be expressed in a displaced form in the patient's outside life. If the optimal line of development of the capacity for concern is recapitulated within the therapy situation, it sometimes is possible to create a genuine capacity for concern, even though this emotion was previously expressed primarily by the patient's false self.

THE DEVELOPMENT OF THE MORAL SENSE

While it has not been among his best-known contributions, Winnicott did make a major addition to a psychoanalytic theory of moral development. Winnicott took a strong stand against a superimposed moral training. In one of his BBC talks, entitled "The Innate Morality of the Baby" (1964c), he said: "This word 'training' always seems to me to be something that belongs to the care of dogs. Dogs do need to be trained . . . but a dog doesn't have to grow up eventually into a human being, so when we come to your baby we have to start again, and the best thing is to see how far we can leave out the word 'training' altogether." Winnicott could be faulted for countering Klein's intrinsically "evil" baby with his "innocent" baby. But he did have strong convictions that the job of the parents is to not interfere with the innate base for an ultimate adult moral sense. His position, however, was not extreme in that direction, as he did believe that morals, values, and culture in general had to be transmitted from generation to generation. But the method of transmission was one of his deepest interests. However, first let us run through this Winnicottian developmental line.

As might be expected, the line begins in the beginning. Winnicott felt that the core of morality was laid down by an empathic, good enough caretaker (he included fathers). The infant is bathed in good care and can help to counter its own intrinsic destructive "bad" parts with the sense of goodness. Admiration of the parents provides a base for linking innate goodness with environmental goodness. A reciprocal relationship is set up, a basis for feeling toward others—as they feel toward you and vice versa. If you know how another person feels and can relate it to feelings you have had yourself, then you don't have to be told how you ought to act toward the other person. Winnicott felt this was the fundamental base of morality.

Another link is the sense of responsibility toward others—he means an intrinsic sense of responsibility, not something you learn from the Ten Commandments. Winnicott felt that once moral imperatives have to be brought in it is too late, unless extensive therapeutic intervention is possible. A natural, developmental sense of responsibility occurs on the way toward the establishment of a sense of concern, as elaborated in the earlier parts of this chapter. Again, if a good enough relationship with the environment-mother and the object-mother is present, and the infant and toddler can give vent to drives that can be felt naturally and reacted to by the object-mother, then the stabilizing, protective relationship with the environment-mother helps this process to continue. Ultimately, as has been explained, there is a merging in the child's eyes of the environment-mother and the object-mother. The system stabilizes and integrates, and there is an optimal cooperation between facilitation and maturation. A by-product of these processes is the capacity of the child to feel the primitive drives, to see their potential for destructiveness, but not to become so terrified that the drives will actually do in the caretaker. This all leads to the child feeling that the drives are real, are his or hers, and that he or she has responsibility for them.

This sense of responsibility is a necessary step in Winnicott's development of a moral sense. The stage of responsibility and concern allows the child to develop the desire for the confidence in and the opportunity for constructive, making-up, reparative activity toward the previously aggressed-against caretaker. Presumably this provides a developmental base for future family and social responsibility and action. Clearly, unless the contributing-in is recognized and validated by the caretaker, the system bogs down and the chance for a higher-level morality is limited. How many social

activists can continue their altruistic activities without some ultimate recognition on the part of society? Taking it back to early
childhood, this is what Winnicott (1964c) said about the time during
which this validation of constructive activity occurs. He referred to

> little contributions to society which only the mother of the baby is
> sensitive enough to appreciate. A smile can contain all this, or a
> clumsy gesture of the arm or a sucking noise indicating readiness for
> a feed. Perhaps there is a whimpering sound by which the sensitive
> mother knows that if she comes quickly she may be able to attend
> personally to a motion which otherwise becomes just a wasted mess.
> This is the very beginning of cooperation and a social sense and is
> worth all the trouble it involves. [p. 94]

Once the basics (the capacity for concern, for contributing-in and
reparations) have been established, the child who has been growing
cognitively is more and more ready for the acquisition of higher-
level morals and values. This brings in the method of this acquisition, referred to earlier. It is quintessentially Winnicottian. In his
paper on "Morals and Education" (1963d), Winnicott wrote: "The
stage becomes set for those engaged in infant-and-child-care to
leave lying round not only objects (such as golliwogs or teddy bears
or dolls or toy engines) but also moral codes. These moral codes are
given in subtle ways by expressions of acceptance or by threats of
withdrawal of love" (p. 99). Winnicott goes on: "There are those
who fear to wait, and who implant, just as there are those who wait,
and keep ready for presentation the ideas and expectations that the
child can use on his arrival at each new developmental stage of
integration and capacity for objective consideration" (p. 100).

Thus, moral codes and values are optimally transmitted in a
manner that dates back developmentally to Winnicott's way of
seeing primary creativity, and later the creation of transitional
objects and phenomena. He makes a crucial point. When the setting
is right, when there is trust, communication, the base for a sense of

responsibility that has been worked at by the family over time, then values are experienced by the child as being there. They are not forced, but apprehended, played with, modified, and presumably, if they are consistent with the developmental base for morality that has already been established, they can be acquired as if they were created by the child him- or herself. And to some extent, they were. Because now we are referring to an older child, the sense that a moral education is not a force feeding gives the child an opportunity to help shape the nature of the value being acquired. The values don't have to come out in the same form as they exist in the parents. In Winnicott's terms, they have been able to enter potential space and be subjected to the creative processes that are present there. One could critically maintain that this is nothing more than progressive education. On one level this is true, but Winnicott's point is built on his whole developmental schema. He is saying more than the fact that love is the way we raise children. He wrote this in "Morals and Education" (1963d):

> In these matters the answer is always that there is *more to be gained from love than from education.* Love here means the totality of infant- and child-care, that which facilitates maturational processes. It includes hate. Education means sanctions and the implantation of parental or social values *apart from* the child's inner growth or maturation. [p. 100]

When Winnicott wrote that love "includes hate," he is not just presenting us with a playful paradox. In his broad sense, parental love and empathy require that the destructive forces be taken into account by the family in a very real manner. It is only through the process that Winnicott has laid out for us that, in his terms, true love and altruism can develop within a real person. Martyrdom isn't necessary in his world.

As we have seen, Winnicott has concerned himself more with the two-person aspects of the development of the moral sense than with the three-person, superego aspects. He does write about the primitive superego, where

> the infant's and the small child's innate moral code has a quality so fierce, so crude, and so crippling. . . . The infant suffers talion fears. The child bites in an excited experience of relating to a good object, and the object is felt to be a biting object. The child enjoys an excretory orgy and the world fills with water that drowns and with filth that buries. [p. 101]

This innate "primitivity" must be civilized by the environment. "These crude fears become humanized chiefly through each child's experiences in relation to the parents, who disapprove and are angry but do not bite and drown and burn the child in retaliation related exactly to the child's impulse or fantasy" (p. 101). In some ways this does not say too much more than Freud's (1910) general theme of taming the instincts, but it does, when taken in conjunction with Winnicott's whole schema, fill in some of the details of an important developmental line.

Winnicott does also say something about God. Again, the theme is similar. If God is superimposed from without, he (or she) is a false god. Winnicott feels that "family gods" are necessary before the idea of a more universal God can be accepted in a meaningful way. He deplores the ideas of the "implanted" god concept.

More and more, some psychoanalysts (Meissner 1984, Rizzuto 1981) and theologians have found Winnicott's concepts of illusion helpful in evolving a developmental view of the process of faith. These efforts have brought seeming incompatibilities between psychoanalysis and religion to a point where a psychoanalysis of religious faith is now more than a reductionistic, negative exercise. Winnicott and those who have used his ideas in this area have for the most part avoided the ontological issue of whether or not there *is* a God and have concentrated on the *experience* of belief and faith.

THE DEVELOPMENT OF THE CAPACITY
TO USE THE OBJECT

This crucial Winnicottian concept has been discussed throughout Chapter 5, since the realistic delineation of the self cannot be separated from that of the object. This concept is of pivotal importance in development and in therapy. Winnicott's "using" someone else refers to a healthy usage. When you are in a reasonable, equal, reciprocal relationship with others, then asking advice, occasionally borrowing something including money, relying on another person's resources of time when you are in need are not necessarily taking advantage of friends. Similarly, a therapist and a patient, if a therapy has been successful, have learned how to, and *have been* using each other. The patient uses the therapist's training and psychological strength, including the therapist's own treatment. The therapist uses the patient for his or her respect, sometimes adulation, money, companionship, and, not infrequently, inspiration. All this is when things are going well. When this state of affairs is not present, Winnicott's delineation of the development of the ability to use the object, which includes a realistic knowing of the object's resources and vulnerabilities, can be useful to the therapist. This is probably one of Winnicott's greatest contributions, but, unfortunately, one that is often easily misunderstood and taken out of context.

THE DEVELOPMENT OF A SENSE OF BELONGING

This is not a developmental line that Winnicott specifically spelled out, but one that is implied in the body of his work. The adult's capacity to feel that he or she belongs is most important. Of course, it is subject to the vicissitudes of the individual's unique social situation. However, in a manner similar to that described in Chapter 5 in the section on the quality of self-possession, the sense of belonging probably has an early developmental baseline.

One way of looking at this is to think of the extreme alternatives:

being possessed or feeling utterly alone. Here we are in Winnicottian territory. His concept of the capacity to be alone (in the
presence of another) helps us to understand the developmental
steps necessary to help prevent the sense of existential aloneness.
Feeling "possessed" is a little more complex. For a moment let us
return to Winnicott's first possession, the transitional object. Here a
belonging that has me/not-me qualities to it differentiates out of the
more intense feeling of being part of and hence belonging *to* the
caretaker. Possession begins to move toward sharing, and transitional space and the transitional process can help to establish a
model for an *illusion* of possession that tends to include the qualities
of belonging. Belonging does not preclude sharing. Clearly I am
referring not only to external objects but to internal ones as well.
Having the latter possess us is quite different from feeling they
belong to us and we to them.

Thus, the important existential feelings of belonging and having
belongings seem to imply a successful negotiation of Winnicott's
early stages, the establishment of a reliable transitional process, and
the capacity for illusion—a "small order," but one that we are
constantly working at in ourselves, and our loved ones, and our
patients.

7

The Development of the Intermediate World and Its Relationship to Creativity

In the last two chapters I have shown how Winnicott's contributions lend themselves to and were conceived according to an organization based on developmental lines. This chapter takes one facet of these interweaving, interrelated lines and teases out the one for which he has been best known and represents his most important and most useful concept. We will be concerned with its applications to therapy and analysis in Chapter 9, but, as has been already alluded to, there are many allied fields where Winnicott's intermediate world and its implications for development help inform our knowledge of the acquisition of symbolic thinking, language formation, culture, creativity, and ritual formation.

This is a developmental line that proceeds on a long journey. On one level, one could describe it as progressing from the pacifier to the symbolic world, a journey that may not be so long chronologically but surely signifies a transcendent, giant leap. A summary of an example of a specific developmental line (which I have written of previously [Grolnick 1986]) will serve as an illustration. The nineteenth-century novelist George Sand wrote a fascinating au-

tobiography, *Histoire de Ma Vie* (1854), in which she unknowingly
traced out an essentially progressive line of the development of her
intermediate, often secret and, ultimately, creative world. She was
told that when she was an infant someone in the family placed a
small toy lyre on her crib within her reach. She apparently would
strum on the strings and put herself to sleep with the resulting
musical sounds. Then, during what we would now consider her
latency years, she found that she was not alone. An echo seemed to
accompany her in her loneliness:

> I studied this phenomenon with an extreme pleasure. What struck
> me as most strange was to hear my own name repeated by my own
> voice. Then there occurred to me an odd explanation. I thought that
> I was double, and that there was round about me another "I" whom
> I could not see, but who always saw me, since he always answered
> me. [p. 496]

This male auditory imaginary companion was most helpful to her
in coping with her father's death and visits from what she called the
"King of Terrors." The relationship with her mother had always
been deeply ambivalent, and clearly she was thrown into grief over
the loss of an actual father and a potential mother. Eventually Sand
realized, "My mother does not love me as much as I love her."

Life circumstances forced the early adolescent George Sand to
separate from her mother and live with a rather serious-minded
grandmother. She was thrown to her own devices, principally her
fertile imagination, which could induce illusions, often spatial in
nature.

> I lost all notion of reality, and believed I could see the trees, the
> water, the rocks—a vast country—and the sky, now bright, now
> laden with clouds which were about to burst and increase the danger
> of crossing the river. In what a vast space children think they are

acting, when they thus walk from table to bed, from the fireplace to the door. [p. 501]

These passages were culled from Sand's autobiography by James Sully (1906), a creative child psychiatrist at the turn of the century, who wrote *Studies of Childhood,* a book Freud referred to several times. Sully, anticipating Winnicott's spatial sense of psychological view of the imagination, had called the play of the imagination a "region" of a child's life.

As happens in adolescence, externalization occurs both developmentally and defensively, and George Sand created a private religion with its own secret shrine in the woods. The god was called Corambé, a sexual ideal figure who had "all the attributes of physical and moral beauty, the gift of eloquence, the omnipotent charm of the arts—above all the magic of musical improvisation. . . ." Sand created a shrine to which she brought offerings to Corambé, many of these consisting of what eventually became nearly a thousand songs she created for him in the sacred books of this private religion. She found comfort and delight with Corambé. When a male friend sought her out one day and stumbled upon her sacred world, she was crushed: "I destroyed the temple with as much care as I had built it."

Corambé clearly remained buried in the woods, both the actual woods surrounding her home and the imaginative woods of her mind. Through speculation about another version of Corambé, and, yes, of Echo, and yes too, of the little toy lyre on her crib, it would seem that the historical progression experienced by George Sand was tied in with her creative life and its particular qualities, as well as with her ways of dealing with ambivalence and loss and diffusion of sexual identity. She took on a male name, dressed as a male, and ultimately chose the esthenic, ill genius we all know as Chopin!

It is well known that creative people tend to have more instances of delayed transitional objects and phenomena and tend to experi-

ence imaginary companions and doubles (Rank 1914) more frequently than the average individual. The vicissitudes of the transitional world as it unfolds historically seem to have significant
effects on the creative life of the individual and on his or her object
relations.

Having given this dramatic and evocative example gleaned from
George Sand's autobiography, it is time now to outline and detail
what each of us progresses through to a greater or lesser degree.
But what is the beginning, what is the genesis of this phenomenon
that seems to indwell our very illusory and spiritual life? In a way,
without dealing with ontological issues, we are asking about the
origins of our psychological gods.

PRIMARY CREATIVITY

Winnicott seemed to say that in the beginning of this developmental
line, there was primary creativity. This experience emerges out of
the infant's experience of being fused with the mother and from the
mother's empathic capacity and ability to identify with this infant
experience. During the negotiations between this dual unity, at first
the infant shows primarily biological needs—hunger, the need for
comfort and holding—and the mother is often right there. Within
the sense of a classical psychoanalytic infantile omnipotence (Ferenczi 1913), the mother's empathic response experiences the infant's sense of omnipotence. The infant feels a magical ability to
create the experience of satisfaction. Winnicott stresses this as not
only a passive experience, but one that is gradually transformed
into an active one. The child begins to provide not only biologically
driven clues for the detecting mother's discernment, but demonstrates what Winnicott called spontaneous gestures. These would
have more to do with comfort and holding, and, almost from the
beginning, the need to *play*. This gestural, preverbal byplay between mother and child, if responded to in an easy, empathic,
bodily manner, can lead to a more intense experience of primary

creativity that the infant can feel he can construct. Of course, these experiences are inferred (as inference is how Winnicott the child analyst developed this helpful concept). Winnicott saw this period of time as the base for a developmentally progressive sense of building the subjective sense of the capacity to be able to create. Missing enough of this experience could lead to the sense of inability to make something new happen and could help reinforce the anticonstructive, yes, destructive forces, culminating in an ultimate sense of impotence with reference to the outer world.

Winnicott implied that primary creativity was a basic infantile need. Without it, the next phase, the infant's internalization of the sense of being able to create, leads to the mother, who by now wants to re-create her own personal world, beginning not to respond to all of the infant's gestural requests. This provides a sense of frustration, thereby helping to foster the separation–individuation process and internalize more and more the infant's sense of a capacity to create.

THE TRANSITIONAL OBJECT
AND TRANSITIONAL PHENOMENA

During the time the mother and infant are increasingly beginning to differentiate themselves as partly separated creatures, the experiences and objects that are shared between them have a me-not me quality to them. They are neither infant nor mother. Of course this is all a gradual shift that never resolves. In one sense, the entire world is experienced as transitional, between the me and not me. Greenacre's (1958) interesting concept of collective alternates takes this into account within the world of heightened perception of the artist. She thought that the artist tended not to develop specific material transitional objects but took the very perceptual world itself as a comforting, bridging entity. In a Western society where infants and children sleep alone without a sibling or parent to hold on to during the perils of the darkness and emptiness of the night, objects and experiences are held on to for comfort while they help complete a sense of body image when the latter is regressed somewhat during the whole experience of sleeping, especially alone. The objects that are historically related to the nursing, feeding, or sleeping situation should have some aspects of those experiences. Transitional objects tend to be soft and are capable of being cuddly; they help to evoke primitive memories of being held, comforted, fed and, importantly, played with. Eventually, probably 70 percent of children in separately bedded situations (Ekecranz and Ruhde 1971) have transitional objects (blankets, diapers, stuffed animals), and probably a significant number have what are termed transitional phenomena. These are perceptual experiences, such as a tune, a mobile, a space on the ceiling, or the crib itself. They cannot be held and controlled as easily as transitional objects themselves, and hence must manifest themselves and influence development in somewhat different ways than transitional objects. Also, there probably are synaesthetic capabilities in creative people. An example is an artistically and poetically talented young woman I once saw in psychotherapy. I could not learn much about her early childhood, but her dramatic adolescence rang out loud and clear. Her father was an alcoholic jazz musician who used to take her into the basement, where he frequently played the piano. He would share his wine with her, let her slip into a somnolent state, run his fingers through her hair, and keep repeating the words "black velvet," the name of a song he played. She would fall asleep this way. Later on, in her twenties, she married an outdoors type who was Caucasian, as she was. In spite of some appealing characteristics, she could not be excited sexually by him. She found that she fantasized about having intercourse with a black man with tight muscles and smooth skin, which she rather readily associated with "black velvet." This was the only way she could have an orgasm. After a while she began to drink and would occasionally go on a binge and frequent bars, where she would pick up black men. She sought out partners who were muscled and smooth-skinned and would then go to bed with them. It is not unusual that the qualities of transitional objects or phenomena (here phenomena, as it was with George Sand) will appear in either object choice or some aspects of the self representation. The synaesthesia occurred in the shift from the verbal "black velvet" to the tactile and textural.

Of course this example takes us from the realm of the transitional into the realm of the fetishistic. This is an important distinction to make. The transitional object should be comforting, usually soft, involved in play that is not deeply instinctualized, and be part of a progressive developmental process that intrinsically involves an interpersonal interaction. When the fetishistic spectrum is involved, the objects tend to be harder, more easily interchangeable, and more or less permanently substituting for body or specifically phallic faults. When a true fetishism is involved, an orgasm is a necessary component of the experience.

Transitional objects should also be differentiated from what Winnicott and subsequently Gaddini (1978) termed precursor objects. These generally precede the formation of a transitional object and are usually parts of the infant's or the mother's body, such as a finger, a thumb, or a part of the mother's skin or mouth or nursing robe. These are clearly direct substitutes for incomplete body image sensations. A precursor object could transform into a transitional object if it becomes embedded in an only partly differentiated, me/not-me, progressive and potentially playful psychological field. Gaddini has shown that traumatic experiences with precursor objects can lead to early psychosomatic symptoms such as rumination, infantile colic, asthma, and self-rocking.

Winnicott saw transitional objects as having an important place in development. Others have felt that transitional objects represented defects in the mother–child interaction and hence were pathological (see Brody 1980, Sperling 1963). However, at this time most of those who work with children and observe them either clinically or scientifically agree that transitional objects are normal manifestations within Western society. That a child can thrive without an apparent transitional object is clear. But to the extent one accepts this Winnicottian developmental line, it seems reasonable to posit that each child will "transitionalize" some part of his or her environment and use it as an adjustor and balancer of the complicated process of separating from while still feeling a bond with the mother. It would seem that only an impossibly ideal mother and child could successfully negotiate this long journey that is milestoned with signs that the mother reads from the culture, and the baby from his or her inner, built-in conflicting experiences that herald autonomy, being left alone, as well as being together (even when the other side of the dyad wants separateness). These signs call for solitary work or play. In the 1940s, they said that "it takes two to tango." Perfect couples are a rarity. Hence the blanket and the teddy bear to the rescue! When Mother and Father are preoccupied with a squabble, or with their own need for another kind of love, what's the harm if the toddler nestles up with his or her favorite imaginative, loved object and is transported into a self-created, other world? This is a world with images, smells, and feels of mother and, for a time, it will do. If left too long in that state, trouble begins; the imaginative world can become an end in itself rather than a necessary adaptive detour. It is within this context that Winnicott's basic and crucial concept of "good enough" can be understood. Perfect is impossible, and if stimulated, it is false and ultimately destructive, whereas *not* good enough creates deprivation with all of its complications.

EARLIER AND LATER
TRANSITIONAL OBJECTS

It is becoming clear that the long developmental line traveled by the intrapsychic process occurring between reality and fantasy, and (from another vantage point) between self and object relations, means that the transitional object or phenomenon both is, and signifies, different things at different times. Already we have discussed the primitive, precursor objects that can, but do not necessarily do, convert into transitional objects when the intrapsychic and extrapsychic environments are propitious. Then, some of the earliest attachments occurring even at 3 and 4 months of age are laced with sensorimotor "glue." Fred Busch (1974), using careful observational data, chose to differentiate between a first and second transitional object, the former usually being acquired during the first year of life and the latter during the second. Usually the child chooses either one or the other, but not both. Busch felt that it was necessary to have a transitional object for a year or more to call it such. This seems a little arbitrary but does emphasize that the object or phenomenon is important, meaningful, and loved; it is not a fly-by-night affair. As parents have become more tolerant of these little competitors, and actually have begun to see them as helpers, their lifespan has become extended (in normal children), well toward and even into the time of adolescence. Of course, the love affair has become weakened and the need for its replenishment is manifesting itself in shorter and shorter liaisons.

Busch defined the criteria for the first transitional object. The timing was during the first year; separation from the mother and the regressive experience of sleep are crucial instigators; the duration is at least one year; there is a need for it to function as a soother in order to decrease anxiety (while a fetishistic object should *increase* it); drive satisfaction, particularly the oral drive, is only a minor part of the attachment; the object seems to be chosen by the child amongst a number of possibilities rather than being given to or even forced on him or her, such as in the instance of the pacifier; and the object should not be a part of the child's body. Essentially, the first transitional object—or, one could say, an early one—is an indicator of a movement away from more attachment behaviors and symbiotic states of mind toward early differentiation and separation. The transitional object cannot come alive until the infant's mind is capable of the perceptual and emotional job of creating boundaries and differentiating itself as an entity. The child is on its transcendent journey from recognition memory to more and more evocative memory, where the nurturing modality can be spontaneously evoked in its absence. There is a long, gradual, and spiraling pathway toward this indefinite ending by the beginning of the fourth year of life, as Mahler and colleagues described it (1975).

It should be evident that transitional objects acquired during the second year of life are more sophisticated than their first-year counterparts in a manner analogous to the vast differences between the 6-month-old and the toddler. When a nonhuman object is brought into or arises from the world of a partially differentiated and partly separated self and object rapprochement-oriented psychological field, it is serving continued but now transcendentally different functions for the child, and for the mother for that matter.

Some of this is epitomized in an example Greenacre once cited. It was about a little boy who was afraid of the dark and of a particular closet in his room. He mastered his fear by throwing his treasured blanket before him into the closet and then, with the area scouted out and declared safe by his friend, he could enter. Here the child is using the transitional object to master, explore, and establish boundaries. The blanket can now be given up temporarily in a more cavalier manner, and the capacity to play alone, as Winnicott put it, is being established. Of course "alone" at that time implies the background safety-net presence of the mother, who can be returned to should an urgent situation arise. In addition, the second year of life, during the time of rapprochement, is a stage of early genital awareness (Galenson and Roiphe 1971). The possibility of gender identification of the object is present, as is the greater ease of its instinctualization. The latter, of course, could lead to subsequent excitatory, instinctualized play and possible negative effects on the developmental acquisition of a creative play and symbolic capacity, as well as the possibility that transitional objects and phenomena could become contaminated by fetishistic components.

THE FATE OF THE
TRANSITIONAL OBJECT

That Winnicott felt that transitional objects ultimately faded away and were transformed into the world of fantasy, play, imagination, creativity, and symbolism is well known. It is now equally well known by those who are familiar with the Winnicott literature that it is generally now accepted, following Tolpin's (1971) lead, that transitional objects do not sublimate away but are gradually internalized into self-soothing, self-assuring, and self-securing, self-evocative structures. Clearly these are not situated in a separate intrapsychic, metaphoric space with reference to the internalizations of the interactions with the principal caretakers. The transitional object helps to facilitate and adjust these interactions so that less conflicted and more reliable internalized capacities associated with nurturing and protecting can be acquired. That children can't be raised only by their teddy bears is obvious, and one needn't bring in the disastrous effects Harlow found when monkeys were raised by cloth surrogate mothers.

Thus, to the extent that one sees the transitional object as a facilitator of development, it serves important, complex functions. Aside from its fostering and participating in the process of internalization, Metcalf and Spitz (1978), for example, saw the appearance of the transitional object as an indicator that the beginnings of evocative memory structures were being laid down. They saw that the transitional object also could serve as a psychic organizer during the progressions from recognition memory to the ultimate establishment of evocative memory (Fraiberg 1969). The transitional object serves as a prosthesis for memory, an outer model for it. In essence, the child can use the blanket to evoke a memory of the mother and "hold" a little longer in her absence. Presumably this facilitates the corresponding development of inner cognitive and affective structures that lead to meaningful evocative memory.

TRANSITIONAL OBJECTS
AND LANGUAGE DEVELOPMENT

The vital step in the child's development occurs in the crux of the movement from the one-word sentence (holophrastic speech) to the discursive, syntactic mode. As Metcalf and Spitz (1978) point out, it is at this time that there is a potential burst of imaginative mental activity, which is not difficult to correlate with Winnicott's more clinical realization of the importance of the vicissitudes of the history of the individual child's transitional object and his or her creative life.

Weich (1968, 1978) has contributed the concept of transitional language to the literature. He pointed to observations of certain toddlers who sometimes "carry" around nonsense, often holophrastic words as if they were transitional objects. These phenomena have multiple meanings and multiple usage. They are suggestive of and reminiscent of what had been called *poetic language* by Jakobson (1960) and the importance of ambiguity (Empson 1930) in the nature of creative imagery and language. Just how transitional language and the capacity for language creativity and language play (Kirschenblatt-Gimblett 1976) articulate (if they do) with each other remains to be worked out by those who are interested in plumbing the depths of the origins of creativity.

INTERMEDIATE SPACE
AND POTENTIAL SPACE

Winnicott tends to use the terms *intermediate space, potential,* and *the third world* (between reality and fantasy) as synonymous. However, a differentiation is implied in his reverting to the usage of potential space in his final, critical book, *Playing and Reality,* which concerns itself so much with the line of development under discussion. Intermediate space best describes the state of affairs when there is a true only partly differentiated self and nonself and when the boundaries between reality and fantasy are only partly established.

This is an early stage of Rose's transitional process (1978, 1980). During this time there is an interacting mix of inner and outer, self and nonself, primary and secondary process, and reality and primitive fantasy. The objects and perceptual experiences, and the very space itself between mother and infant, are crystallizations of this transitional process. The concept is a most helpful one in understanding an idea that is complex and at times difficult to grasp and hold onto. What "transitional process" implies, or rather states, is that during the time of only partial separation and differentiation, *all* perceptual experiences are "transitionalized." The ones that concern us, the ones that become important in the idiosyncratic developmental process in the individual, are precipitated out of this inner and outer flow and continuum and are used for stabilization of the separation–individuation process and to adjust the need for comfort and protection. Some of them become loved, are felt to be special possessions, and can serve to bring the investments and affects they "contain" into the relationship with the nonhuman environment (Searles 1960).

Thus, intermediate space seems a good way to describe the presymbolic space between the me and the not-me. When Winnicott writes of potential space in *Playing and Reality,* he seems to be referring more to symbolic, metaphoric space. One could say that the combination of actuality and primitive fantasy present in intermediate space has been replaced by a more abstract, sophisticated world where symbolic images, including verbal forms, exist. Some writers, such as Deri (1978, 1984), prefer to see this space as more or less synonymous with the preconscious, thus moving back to Freud's topographic theory.

Winnicott's elucidating concept of potential space is a legacy of its more primitive versions in early childhood that might be best termed intermediate space. Both are to be differentiated from Euclidean space. Intermediate space is presymbolic in nature, and potential space is symbolic. Deri, in her interesting and helpful book *Symbolization and Creativity* (1984), shows how difficulties in the good enough fine tuning of the early developmental interfacing between mother and child can lead to defects (especially with constitutional predisposition) in the ability to symbolize in an innovative, creative manner. How many of our patients of varied diagnostic types experience the world and themselves in a bland, concretistic manner. Winnicott repeatedly wrote about helping people who don't know how to play, who can't really free associate, and who require a period of another chance at development before they are able to benefit from more traditional, standard, insight-oriented therapy. The world has to mean something, to be symbolic, before symbolized conflicts can be analyzed. This is a crucial Winnicottian point. (How some of Winnicott's concepts can be used therapeutically toward this end will be discussed further in Chapter 9.)

We are perched here at the interface at what Rose (1978) has called the creativity of everyday life, and the creative process itself. Winnicott called the early transitional object our first illusion—it is not mother, yet it helps the child to build the illusion that it *is* mother. Illusion, used in this healthy sense, has its own developmental line and ultimately can lead to the ability to pretend and to the willing suspension of disbelief that is necessary for an audience to either create, or re-create, a work of art. To the extent that there is a theatrical mode in psychotherapy and psychoanalytic situations, the transference can be seen as a make-believe piece of experience that is necessary in order for the patient to undergo an analytic process.

Fantasies and their narrative forms exist in potential space. An interesting way in which this enters the therapeutic situation occurs in certain patients who entertained some of their most soothing experiences while being told or read fairy tales or stories during the time of going to bed and to sleep. The carry-over is the adult who prefers, and often needs, some television patter or a book to read in order to nod off to sleep.

This can move into the characterological and the pathological when the stories begin to develop a fixated, even fetishistic quality. The example of my patient who was told to "think black velvet" is pertinent here. Another patient transformed the Tarzan stories he was read at night into an elaborate network of solitary fantasies (Volkan [1973] has called these *transitional fantasies*) that included the patient as the Tarzan figure. He made up many adventures that served to comfort him and made him feel safe, whole, and less lonely within a narcissistic family matrix. He could have the illusion that he was in control of some aspect of his life experience. Later on, the Tarzan–Jane stories helped to determine poor object choices, the decision to become a pilot, and to become "high" during many periods of dangerous alcoholic binges that had a strong suicidal component.

IMAGINARY COMPANIONS

From the beginning Winnicott described the imaginary companion as an older relative of early transitional objects. Clearly the infant's mind cannot conjure up a full, well-delineated, friendly imaginary companion until his or her cognitive and affective capacities have matured. Sometimes one can see the process of personalization occurring while watching a mother and a child interact. The blanket can be used by the mother or father as a hand puppet, and then the couple becomes deeply involved in dramatized play. Later on the personality of the blanket can become detached from its origins and begin to exist on its own.

Multiple imaginary companions can occur and, as one might expect, can be the prehistory of a multiple personality disorder. Another possibility is the "imaginary companion à deux." An example is a patient of mine who had a long-standing interest in the theater and participated in amateur productions. She recalled how she and her younger sister both had multiple imaginary companions and how they used to create stories and act them out together.

The term *act out* is being used in a dramatic sense here, but it is clear that it is in a developmental continuum with what might be considered to be more destructive and pathological acting out. (My patient was interested in acting and her sister in acting out.) Winnicott recognized this early on when he pointed out that acting out was a method of communication that often stemmed from early deprivation and that it signified hope (Winnicott 1956a). This also implies that in normal development, externalization onto some part of the external world, whether it be a blanket, a stuffed animal, a make-believe stage, or a real one, is modeled by the transitional object. Healthy living and experiencing or, in other terms, a healthy use of the developmental given of a transitional process involves allowing it to encompass the external world. Magical thinking needs to transform into the magic of the moon and its shadows and the magic of the silver screen, as it once was called.

DREAMING AS A
TRANSITIONAL PHENOMENON

Since dreams have always been mysteries that have been equated with the imagination and the world between the real and the fantasized, it is not surprising that they were important to Winnicott. In his original paper on transitional objects and phenomena (Winnicott 1951), he tended to use them as possible ways an infant could deal with maternal failure, listing them along with fantasying. Then, in a more definitive study of dreaming entitled "Dreaming, Fantasying, and Living" (Winnicott 1971a), he tended to distinguish dreams from fantasying. In the patient he described in that paper, fantasying could only "fill the gap, and this gap was an essential state of doing nothing while she was doing everything" (pp. 29–30). As a young child the patient used fantasying as an escape and as a bypassing of both her reality and her dream life. In essence, Winnicott saw the fantasying as having no symbolic value, as contrasted to a dream, which does.

This is a little confusing, as dreams seem to be able to be in the intermediate, protosymbolic world and to be symbols at the same time. The problem is that Winnicott didn't spell out his findings and ideas in the form of developmental lines. It would seem that daydreams and night dreams could be in a developmental continuum, as Winnicott hinted at in his later paper. He was also beginning to arrive at a fuller understanding of the imagination when he placed dreams and not fantasies in its realm. However, people can use fantasies as transitional phenomena or fetishistic phenomena (as in Winnicott's constantly fantasying patient), and they can use dreaming or the dreaming process in the same way. If a person is capable of symbolizing, the (conscious) fantasies they produce will have symbolic value, as will the associations to their dreams. Winnicott does have a point though, as the *experience* of dreaming is closer to the experience of reality than is the experience of fantasying. And there are many patients who use fantasying in a fetishistic manner. But it is hard to agree with Winnicott's implication that fantasying in itself cannot be a symbolic activity. Volkan (1973) discusses a patient with transitional fantasies in a paper that helps to elucidate this important concept that Winnicott brought to our attention but did not elaborate upon sufficiently.

There are reports of two patients who used dreams as transitional phenomena, although, to be more accurate, this usage had fetishistic aspects to it in both patients (Grolnick 1978, 1986). The first was a young man who remembered his dreams in great detail, to the point that he flooded the analysis with them. There was no time to talk about anything else. Attempts to make the standard resistance interpretations only intensified the process. When I ultimately began to understand that the patient used his father's nighttime stories and ultimately his own dreams as transitional and fetishistic phenomena to deal with his terror of the night and nothingness (related to difficulties in early development with his mother), interpretations that took into account the developmental and adaptive nature of the dreams were more effective in slowing down the flow.

This patient was literally terrified of having what he experienced as a dreamless night. It was like a void without any stepping-stones to cross it. There was also evidence that the patient not only used the dreaming process, but specific images in the dream, as transitional phenomena.

Another patient, a borderline, alcoholic woman in once-a-week psychotherapy, kept her television set on every night to help fight her terror of being alone. One day the set broke and she desperately sought out some way of repairing it so she would have it available to her that evening. Unfortunately her plans did not work out, and she was forced to face the night without her "companion." She ultimately fell asleep and awoke, realizing that she had experienced a dream that she had not remembered since her childhood. It had been recurrent, about two or three nights a week. She described it as uncannily beautiful, an abstract synaesthetic, shimmering vortex image that emitted aesthetically pleasing and comforting colors, lines, and musical sounds. She recalled how she used to look forward to this dream and how she used it as a comforter in the midst of a chaotic family life in which she was physically and sexually abused.

To infants and toddlers, dreams are not distinguished from reality and clearly can become important factors influencing the developmental process (Grolnick 1978, Mack 1965). Metcalf and Spitz (1978) described what they term *protodreams* during the first year of life and relate these to transitional phenomena. As the dreaming (and daydreaming) processes move up the developmental line in any one individual, they serve different functions and gradually, if development thrives, move from the protosymbolic to the symbolic mode. It seems reasonable, just as with my television-deprived patient, that during adult times of stress and deprivation, earlier stages can be invoked to provide temporary relief. As such, this is another important developmental line that Winnicott attempted to describe. It crisscrosses so many other lines of development in such complex ways that it is left to others to further elaborate on what Winnicott has begun.

This chapter has covered one of Winnicott's richest and most evocative developmental lines. It has vast implications and applications. The intermediate world described by Winnicott is not only synchronic, as in the willful suspension of disbelief, but is very much diachronic—it is a vital developmental line that begins to tell us something more about the way symbolic activity, imaginative activity, and creativity grow from our earliest months and years.

8

Reading
Winnicott

A READING DIALOGUE

Many readers have trouble reading Winnicott. No doubt one can't be taught to read Winnicott any better than one does naturally. The corollary is that it is pretentious to write a chapter entitled "Reading Winnicott." This is the same issue that beset the Zen scholar, Daisetz Suzuki, who wrote so well on Zen history, practice, philosophy, and phenomenology. However, true Zen followers criticized Suzuki, as they felt it was obvious that authentic Zen experiencing is incompatible with writing about it, as the writing forced the subject into the intellectualized mode.

The solution parallels Winnicott's attempts to deal with his position as being the Dr. Spock of England while at the same time maintaining that one cannot instruct a mother how to mother. The concept of *facilitation* comes to the rescue here. By providing a setting that has certain structure and, seemingly paradoxically, allowing a background sense of freedom and openness, the infant and child, and the infant and child part of the mother, can emerge and even thrive. So really, this chapter should be entitled "Facilitating the Reading of Winnicott," and if it becomes teachy, please discount it, work around it, and in true Winnicottian fashion, you have permission to move to the next chapter and read on. In keeping with modern reader-response literary critical theory, the process of reading is not unlike the complex process of living. In the back of my mind, as I write these sentences, is the idea that the dialogue I am creating with the reader can serve a double purpose—say something about reading Winnicott but also provide a living example of a Winnicottian dialogue, where the mother–therapist–author can be aggressed against, destroyed, yet still exists. I am really doing more than facilitating, yet I think I am facilitating. But that is why the capacity to entertain paradox is so helpful in reading Winnicott, in reading this author, in rearing children, and in being a therapist.

OUT OF CHAOS

In Chapter 2 I cited Marion Milner's memory of Winnicott saying, "What you get out of me you will have to pick out of chaos." However, anyone who claims that he speaks and writes chaotically cannot be very chaotic. I suspect it was part of Winnicott's *false self* to think of himself as teaching down to the nitty-gritty of chaos. It is ironic, but revealing and significant, that the definition of chaos in the *Encyclopaedia Britannica* (1954) stresses that in the Hesiodic theogony, Chaos was not mere vacuum, but filled with clouds and darkness. In later Roman usage, chaos was contrasted with cosmos (the orderly universe). In this sense, chaos has various meanings, the first listed being "the space between heaven and earth." This is not too far removed from Winnicott's potential space, the creative space *between* reality and fantasy.

In this sense, Winnicott's *chaos* is less structured than the writings of, say, Freud, Brenner, and Arlow. But there *is* order, and that order pervades his entire body of writing. Winnicott repeats, reworks, and, in a way most like Freud, is always involved in moving on to new levels of understanding, while he leaves the older, bypassed ideas in his path. This leaves it, in turn, to the reader to place it all in perspective. A historical sense helps, as Winnicott's thinking represents a line of his own development as he writes about the various lines of development that occur throughout the life cycle.

WINNICOTT'S INTELLECTUAL SOURCES

In Chapter 2 I attempted to show the dialectic Winnicott engaged in with his principal intellectual mentors who became his ultimate foils. His writings testify to that state of affairs. It is clear that it became important for him to show his Freudian roots and not present himself as a radical, even though as his final years approached, his psychoanalytic radicalism gradually became more forthright. Prior to that, his ambivalence often leaked out. He was able to acknowledge in letters (Rodman 1987) to James Strachey and Ernest Jones his reluctance to read Freud and the classical psychoanalytic literature. The effects of this struggle with Freud and Klein were twofold. In his earlier writings, Winnicott was truly immersed in ego psychological, structural, drive-oriented psychoanalysis. When he wrote of the ego, he meant ego in terms of Freud's post-1923 structural theory of the ego, id, and superego. However, from the 1960s on, for Winnicott ego began to have meanings that were closer to self-representation, and, ultimately, to a self that resembles the self of Kohut's (1971) self psychology. Winnicott's id began classically as the psychological representation of unconscious biologically driven drives, but sometimes ended up in his later writings more as affect. Even early on, when he (too apologetically I believe) was working with his research analyses with borderline and psychotic patients, on occasion he used love and hate in more of the sense of affects than drives. This is clear in his well-known essay "Hate in the Countertransference," which was published in 1947, when Klein's influence on him was in full sway. In this paper, as in others related to early aggression, guilt, reparations (a Kleinian concept), and the capacity for concern, when Winnicott writes of early development, he refers to biologically derived drives. In his *ruthless* stage, the *object-mother,* in contrast to the ego-oriented *environment-mother,* is subject to the mercilessness of the infant's aggressive drives. Winnicott follows classical and, in turn, Kleinian theory here. A drive is a drive is a drive. But in describing the adult situation, especially within the therapeutic setting, hatred in the therapist often seems to be more a patient-provoked *affect* than a drive. Winnicott doesn't tend to identify it as an affect, as would Kernberg in contemporary psychoanalysis.

It should be said, however, that when we read him carefully Winnicott can be quite modern in this area. He felt, again in keeping with Kernberg, that for a true drive to exist there must be concomitant development of ego structure. As we know, Winnicott called the stage prior to this development the *pre-ruth* stage, when infantile destructiveness is not intentional and basically incidental. It is this pre-ruth time that Kernberg probably would describe as concerning primitive affects. Again, both would agree that the id requires adequate ego development to be epistemologically at the level of a drive. In sum, I do think that the reader must always look at the context when Winnicott uses the terms id, aggression, ruth, and hate.

In deference to his allegiance to Klein, Winnicott retained the concepts of the depressive position, reparations, manic defense, and so on. These concepts were reasonably compatible with his brand of object relations theory. However, it is important for the Winnicott student to know that something transcendent happened between Winnicott and Klein following the publication of his famous paper "Transitional Objects and Transitional Phenomena" in the middle of 1951. Winnicott's bombshell was included in one of his footnotes. Phyllis Grosskurth (1986), in her biography of Melanie Klein, describes the interaction. In this footnote Winnicott tried to be conciliator and talked of the possibility of a bridge between the narratives of early infantile development as told by Klein and Anna Freud. Then he added the crucial last line of the footnote: "The only difference left is one of dates, which is in fact an unimportant difference which will automatically disappear in the course of time" (Winnicott 1951, p. 239).

While it is true that Klein's early phases and mechanisms have now been revisionistically advanced up the developmental time-table, in 1951 Klein did not think the time issue was trivial. She firmly believed that the major developmental events, the paranoid position, the depressive position, manic defense, reparations, and the Oedipus complex basically played themselves out during the first six months of life. The last line of the footnote became the essential ending of the bilateral collegiality between Klein and Winnicott. She never again warmed up to him, although he always retained his awe of and respect for her, as is evident in the Kleinian flavor to even some of his later papers. Grosskurth (1986) reports that the English analyst John Padel suggested, "I don't think that one can truly understand his papers unless one is aware that they have that secondary air of getting her to modify something."

ACKNOWLEDGING THE WORK OF OTHERS

The Winnicott reader should be aware that Winnicott's works are not annotated and referenced in the reasonably scholarly manner we expect in the Freudian literature. Winnicott seemed too impatient to spend much time looking up citations and creating an impeccable bibliography. This is evident from the contribution made by one of his most influential followers, Masud Khan. Khan helped Winnicott edit and contributed a detailed conceptual index to *The Maturational Processes and the Facilitating Environment*. In the acknowledgment section, Winnicott made a revealing statement when referring to Khan: "He is responsible for my gradually coming to see the relationship of my work to that of other analysts, past and present." It's not that Winnicott did not want to acknowledge his predecessors and contemporaries. I believe he lived in a world of ideas that he experienced, in characteristic Winnicottian fashion, as intermediate between himself and others. He was explicit about this in the same preface to *The Maturational Processes and the Facilitating Environment:*

> First I wish to acknowledge my debt to my psychoanalytic col-
> leagues. I have grown up as a member of this group, and after so
> many years of inter-relating it is now impossible to me to know what
> I have learned and what I have contributed. The writings of any one
> of us must be to some extent plagiaristic. Nevertheless I think we do
> not copy; we work and observe and think and discover, even if it can
> be shown that what we discover has been discovered before.

What can the reader do? Try to take in Winnicott's ideas and the ideas of his intellectual environment, add the ingredient of the state of mind of this impressionistic psychoanalytic creator, and you may be tuned in sufficiently to be able to fill in the missing spaces and place Winnicott in an intellectual, historical perspective. The reader should be reminded that Winnicott read literature and poetry extensively and wrote his own poetry. He was a man steeped in Western culture and ideas, but not compulsive enough to tie in for the reader his important historical, literary, critical, philosophical, and aesthetic antecedents and fellow travelers.

WINNICOTT ON DIAGNOSIS AND PROGNOSIS

As is evident, Winnicott was not interested in stereotyping. His was not a fixed world of diagnostic entities in the sense that official classifications held no fascination for him. I think it is fair to say that he was Kierkegaardian and that between *being,* which is first necessary, and *doing,* which makes one feel real, there is an intermediate, yet transitional state of *becoming.* The therapist and the patient do not start, and should not start, as fixed entities. Thus Winnicott had a relativistic sense of diagnosis. He had to use some jargon and orient the reader; but roughly, psychosis is psychosis and borderline is borderline. It falls to the reader to extrapolate Winnicott's diagnostic hints to his or her own patients. But the caveat is always there—don't prematurely close off a diagnosis with its inevitable influence on the method of treatment and prognosis. Prognosis was also open-ended.

Winnicott tended to take on patients who were extremely difficult. He often saw others' failures and patients who felt hopeless. Once he told a patient that he agreed with the depressed man's sense that he was hopeless, but that he would treat him nevertheless. The patient experienced hope for the first time. So the reader would be aided by giving Winnicott the benefit of the doubt—not dubbing him an optimist or a pessimist. He worked nonselectively with patients he saw and tried his best to help them, using whatever he had learned from his training and from his life. If at times he blurred the distinction between psychoanalysis and psychotherapy, he warrants our forgiveness.

WINNICOTT, FATHERS, AND FEMINISM

As feminist critics become aware of Winnicott's importance as a Freudian, as a philosophically minded psychologist, as a social commentator and propagandist, his attitudes toward women and men are being looked at more carefully. There is no question that he stressed the role of the mother, and although he often acknowledged the father's importance in the infant's early development, it was *not* stressed. Perhaps his credo could be read into a statement he made in the introduction to *The Child, the Family and the Outside World* (1964d): ". . . everyone who is sane, everyone who feels himself to be a person in the world, and for whom the world means something, every happy person, is in infinite debt to a woman" (p. 10). Basically he felt that the early maternal relationship was crucial. That mothering instincts in men are powerful he knew—he lived it out with his patients. But the feminist movement was not at a sophisticated point when he was in his most productive years, and it certainly hadn't influenced the culture to the point that a less economically potent male staying home with the children while mother worked was an acceptable situation. I think the reader can fault Winnicott for, on one level, raising mothers to the heights, but at another, keeping them close to home and hearth. The whole issue could be passed off merely by stating that Winnicott was a man of his time, and inevitably he reflected contemporary male attitudes. But Winnicott demands more criticism because he was a man ahead of his time. He consciously saw woman as one of the early primitive gods, and gave her pride in her biological and psychological creativity and empathic capacity. He felt the presence of each sex in the other, *cross-identifications* as he termed it. About his unconscious hatred of women, let the reader decide.

When it came to penis envy, Winnicott was somewhat reductionistically early Freudian. In the recently published draft of a talk, "This Feminism," that he gave to the Progressive League in 1964 (Winnicott 1964), he spelled out what he felt. After referring to the fantasies of the phallic woman in both males and females, he wrote:

> Here is a root of feminism. I cannot help it if there is much else in feminism, and if logic can be brought in on the side of much that feminism does and says. The root of it lies in the general delusion, *in girls and also in men,* that there is a female penis, and in the special fixation of certain women and men at the phallic level, that is, at the stage before the attainment of full genitality. [p. 187—Winnicott's italics]

Winnicott found it necessary to follow this with his reassurance to women that male envy for women is more powerful than penis envy. Again, the reader must enter into a dialogue with Winnicott, taking into account the early feminist time in which he worked; the issue of how much penis envy is a metaphor and how much it operates at an anatomical level is still being debated in psychoanalytic circles.

It has been pointed out (Hodges 1987) that Winnicott's well-meaning and exceptionally popular BBC broadcasts were either consciously or unconsciously in the service of the British government's need to help the wartime working woman to relinquish her position to the returning heroes and to retreat to home and children. I don't doubt that Winnicott's mother worship influenced his position on the social and political level and that he probably would never have been a card-carrying feminist. However, Winnicott's omission of the mothering father was, in part, due to the fact that basically he was always writing about the caretaking function and how it interacts with early infant development. Winnicott had so much to say to us about this that it would be presumptuous to insist that he rise above his time and his own psychology.

WINNICOTT'S USE OF WORDS

That Winnicott had a poet's way with words should be self-evident to most of his readers. It is also clear, but deserves emphasis, that he used words themselves to arrive at innovative concepts. This is in keeping with Wittgenstein's premise that basic ideas are derived from play with language. Winnicott played with words, psychoanalytic and otherwise. I have already mentioned that he created from ruthlessness the stage of *ruth* and then the time of formless *pre-ruth*. *Depersonalization*, the diagnostic and descriptive term, is turned around into a powerful Winnicott concept, *personalization*, the process of creating a person immanent within a psychosomatic matrix. Then integration is not only contrasted with *disintegration* but with *unintegration*, a developmentally natural state that precedes integration, which can be returned to derivatively for rest and refueling when the need to use the energy to pull together and integrate is not necessary. This can occur when the individual is being held by the environmental mother surrogate and there is a chance for in-touchness with the inner self. This is contrasted with his use of *disintegration* as a regressive defense formation. Similarly, the concept of *deprivation,* which we tend to see as primary in nature, is contrasted with *privation.* To be *de*prived, one must have had something positive in the first place.

This playing with word forms and meanings also seemed to help Winnicott to work out his way of seeing the *antisocial tendency.* For Winnicott, action, even what we would call acting out or delinquency, implies hope. *True* privation dictates withdrawal, and, in contrast to the antisocial adolescent, withdrawal does not demand potentially healing action from the environment. As Winnicott put it (Winnicott 1963d, p. 104), "The child knows in his bones that it is *hope* that is locked up in the wicked behaviour, and that *despair* is linked with compliance and false socialization."

In sum, reading Winnicott is not like reading poetry, as some skeptics claim, but it is also not like not reading poetry. It is like the Emily Dickinson scholar who found herself having to reread all 1,775 of Emily's poems each time she was forced to have a hiatus in her study of the poet. With writers like Winnicott who interplay the light and shadow of ideas and feelings, a hermeneutic circle prevails (where one cannot understand the whole without parts or the parts without the whole). Since his work is a backdrop for the therapist and not at all a manual, and since his basic stance to the patient is that of a facilitating representative of the milieu, developing the ability to suspend disbelief (while retaining critical skepticism) and being an open receptor is good training for the reader-therapist.

9

How to Do Winnicottian Therapy

A chapter on technique does not belong in a book on Winnicott. The concept of technique implies a rigor, the adherence to a body of certain rules, and an attempt to achieve a perfection of execution. It implies training as opposed to liberal, open education. How can we mix a Winnicottian emphasis on creativity, having the freedom to make mistakes, with technique? We can't. Yet we, his followers, or those who want to use some of what he had to offer, can, and must, think out what the artist, Winnicott, did in terms of technique and guidelines (we can do away with rules here).

Imagine a fantasied Winnicott trying in one session to teach his method to an aspiring therapist, really an absurdity. Perhaps this is the way to approach the problem of a chapter on Winnicottian technique. This fantasied Winnicott would show the student his office. It would have chairs, a couch, a floor, ceiling, walls, decorations, drapes, or shades. But to Winnicott it is a setting, a potential space. Perhaps another way of putting it is to see it as a theater or stage upon which the drama of psychotherapy or psychoanalysis is played out. Winnicott would say the patient could be on the couch, in the chair, pacing the room, or even lying or sitting on the floor. What is happening between the two people takes precedence over the method one is using. Of course, for analysis, the couch is best. There are reasons for this that will be discussed later.

The student therapist might be told to keep his or her psychoanalytic knowledge in back of his or her mind. A model of development, even the images of a mother and a baby, or a toddler, or a child may come closer to the surface. The therapist might try to let him- or herself oscillate between feeling merged with and separate from the patient (the patient as subjective object versus the patient as objectively perceived).

The therapist must know what's going on, where the patient is on the developmental and diagnostic scale. But the therapist must get in touch with the patient. But not too fast—slowly, slowly as Winnicott advises. Don't impinge on fragile boundaries or carefully hidden away, frightened authentic selves within your patients.

Perhaps Winnicott might say:

Therapist, even with all this responsibility, relax. After all, you are only a facilitator, not prime mover. You can't (and shouldn't) be perfect. You have to make mistakes, which, when worked out between you and the patient, help toward creating the deepest change. You can be angry at the patient. If you never are, go for help!

Don't let yourself be destroyed or demoralized by patients who are trying to foster their own development when they attack or deprecate you.

Relax; it's only therapy—but it's real at the same time, and patients suffer unthinkable anxieties. So do you—or so you did. Try to get in touch with them. Any of us can go crazy. You are the patient's equal, but at the same time, you are the steady, concerned, earnest thinking and feeling professional, flappable sometimes, but essentially unshakable.

You should be able to enjoy this work—because so much of it is play. Hard play in the beginning, but, hopefully if things go well, lighter and more symbolic play later on. Oh, by the way, don't try to show the patient how smart you are, you are good enough. Acting like a smart aleck won't help. And sometimes it is necessary to keep quiet and leave the patient alone, and not insist that every little thing means something (even though deep down you think it does).

Maybe there are too many instructions already. Take what I say with a grain of salt, and go out there and try it. Let me know what happens (we can make that into supervision if you want).

Now my one-lesson Winnicott fantasy must come to earth. Maybe it isn't a fantasy but an illusion, in Winnicott's sense of that word. If a therapist is an original therapist, that is, he or she was held well, handled well, presented to the world in a well-timed manner, and forced to deal with the disillusionments life always offers (unless we are too protected); if a therapist's capacity to be in touch with his or her soma hasn't been discouraged; if a therapist's innate creativity hasn't been squelched by various trainers, ranging from parents to psychotherapy supervisors; if a therapist is blessed by having navigated the world of development optimally, then perhaps one lesson in how to do therapy would work. Most of us have to struggle, learn from the creative process of trial and error, and learn from the working out of failures with the patient. Learning from reading Winnicott, or this chapter, helps, but doing therapy is the best supervisor (even though for a good while a supervisor is good to have). Winnicott's guidelines and, above all, his permissions (it's okay to play, it's okay not to analyze everything, it's okay to hate your patient, etc.) do provide a facilitating setting for the therapist that is analogous to the setting the therapist provides for the patient.

An important guiding image, alluded to above, is that of the mother and baby. Read in Winnicott "mother" and replace her with "therapist." Read "baby" and replace it with "patient." It works, most of the time. To the extent that the therapist has diagnosed the therapeutic field as a developmental one, and to the extent that he

or she conceptualizes the therapeutic situation as a new developmental stage (Loewald 1960), when they don't know what to do,
they can think out the maternal situation and use it as a model. Of
course babies and patients are different. But there are baby stages in
patients (and in therapists) that must be dealt with in not the same,
but in an analogous manner. An experiential as well as a cognitive
understanding of development can facilitate the therapist's facilitation of a patient's development when that development has hit a
snag due to environmental failure or mix-up (Balint 1968). Beware,
however; this model may not work for the psychoneurotic patient
where development was able to proceed well, the intrapsychic
world is well peopled and well integrated, and where the creative
symbolic processes have built those semiotic nuisances we call
neurotic symptoms and inhibitions. Sigmund Freud, Anna Freud,
and the ego psychologists are better teachers where conflict and
advanced rather than primitive defense mechanisms prevail and
earlier stages of development are used defensively. However, in the
author's clinical experience, he has rarely treated a patient who has
not had some developmental difficulty and some experience with
the unthinkable and annihilation anxieties that didn't need tending
to at some point in the therapy or analysis. As Winnicott noted, the
well-equipped therapist can move back and forth between both
developmental levels and diagnostic entities. He, and this chapter,
are geared more to patients who have suffered deeply from the
woes coming from vicissitudes of the developmental process, where
internalization and object and self constancy have not set in adequately and where the integration of the psyche and the soma have
not occurred optimally.

FIELDS OF PERSONS AND DRAMA

To move more toward the specific, let me allude to some of the
qualities of the Winnicottian therapeutic field. As it is an object
relations oriented field, it is personified. Internal and external ob-

jects, transitions between them, constant and inconstant objects are the images that lead to understanding and toward interpretation. As Friedman (1988) has suggested, contemporary patients are assaulting therapists with primitive defenses, anxieties, rages, and raw thrusts of eros, that is, therapists are seeing and treating more borderline, narcissistic, and psychotic patients. A personified, simpler (than orthodox) theory seems to be more attractive and of more assistance to the therapist. Such a theory helps to provide a relatively experience close system to hold onto to help face the onslaught of the patient's primitivity. In a more specifically Winnicottian object relations field, when the time is right and the patient ready, the personifications and the persons can play and interplay. It is this play, and setting up the playground when the patient is not ready, that tries to further the missed developmental play, and interplay, that led to the developmental difficulty in the first place. In sum, the particular level of play that is called for by the patient's needs (nursery presymbolic play, or symbolic play) is facilitated by a personified theory that cries out for a setting or stage to be built for it (Grolnick 1984, Loewald 1975, McDougall 1982, Winnicott 1971a). The theater is improvisational, but as in good improvisational theater, there are overlying meta guidelines and outer limits. There must be a rationale, a reason, in a sense a plot or series of plots, to carry the action along. So according to this model, the therapist is a vitally involved, modernist creative player on a basically developmental stage. This is not acting or performing in its pejorative sense. But it is the use of the theater's essential ingredient of illusion that brings the qualities of creative involvement, the capacity for a make-believe transference, and the ability to be real and not real (human and professional) at the same time.

A theatrical model brings along with it one of the essential characteristics of the creative, that of ambiguity (Adler 1989). Aesthetic ambiguity (Empson 1930) has long been recognized as a necessary but not sufficient ingredient of art. Even though the art of therapy and analysis has been always acknowledged, the more scientific models (Hook 1959), such as the experimental and the observational models, have tended to squeeze ambiguity out of the consultation room. It was not unusual for supervisors and teachers to advise that we shouldn't make an interpretation until we were sure it was correct, and when we were, to deliver it in a forthright, declarative manner. Hardly an ambiguous field! In fact, this technique and the concept of the exact interpretation that informed it are just what Winnicott considered to be the indoctrination of (and impingement upon) the patient. Recently Adler (1989) has written of the dangers of "pathological certainty" within a field of psychoanalysis that is characterized by its essential ambiguity. Adler sees this field as compatible with Winnicott's concepts of transitional phenomena, transitional objects, illusion, and play. The advantages of the personalized nursery and theatrical models that Winnicott provides us are that ambiguity, openness, and creativity are seen as essential ingredients of the therapeutic process, rather than attributes that have to be forced into models that have a more positivistic flavor. Thus Winnicott's good enough, less than perfect alternation of gratification and frustration has its ambiguous dimension that allows the therapeutic field to be developmentally sound, yet provide an opportunity to utilize a creative, playing, open milieu that reaches into the patient's inner creative self, rather than providing a pedantic, indoctrinating schoolroom that can only help to perpetuate the false self of the patient and, very possibly, the grandiosity of the therapist.

SUCCEEDING BY FAILING

Before Winnicott, analyses and therapies were either successes or failures, or sometimes they were middling. Then Winnicott said in 1955:

> There builds up an ability of the patient to use the analyst's limited
> successes in adaptation, so that the ego of the patient becomes able

to begin to recall the original failures, all of which were recorded, kept ready. These failures had a disruptive effect at the time, and a treatment of the kind I am describing has gone a long way when the patient is able to take an example of original failure and be angry about it. Only when the patient reaches this point, however, can there be the beginning of reality testing. . . .

The way this change comes about from the experience of anger is a matter that interests me in a special way, as it is at this point in my work that I found myself surprised. The patient makes use of the analyst's failures. [p. 298]

Winnicott goes on to elaborate:

Others may be surprised, as I was, to find that while a gross mistake may do but little harm, a very small error of judgement may produce a big effect. The clue is that the analyst's failure is being used and must be treated as *past* failure, one that the patient can perceive and encompass, and be angry about now. The analyst needs to be able to make use of his failures in terms of their meaning for the patient, and he must if possible account for each failure even if this means a study of his unconscious countertransference. [p. 298]

It should be stressed that Winnicott did not mean planned failures or mistakes. These would lead to an artificial analytic field that could only perpetuate rather than relieve the pressure of these buried caches of previous developmental failures. The therapist can rest assured that empathic and technical errors will come in the natural course of events. It is here that Winnicott differentiates himself from other psychoanalytic innovators who advocated various manipulations of the transference, such as Alexander's advice that the analyst *act* in a manner opposite to that of the original parents. Again, when developmental work is needed, Winnicott advocates setting up a good enough analytic environment, which includes the building of a potential play space in which the successes and failures of both parties can be experienced, worked through, and played through.

There is a similarity between Winnicott's use of failure with Kohut's (1971) way of allowing a buildup of a narcissistic transference and then awaiting analyst's empathic failures, which are to be worked out with the patient in an experential and a cognitive manner. Actually, there is not much difference between Winnicott and the concept that Kohut termed "transmuting internalization." This is the structure-building goal of both Winnicottian and Kohutian therapy. Perhaps the most important difference is timing. Winnicott seems to advocate working with failures earlier in the treatment than Kohut, who required a gradually unfolding, ultimately intense narcissistic transference to occur before failures are negotiated with the patient. There is also an implication in Kohut's work that the analyst should attempt to supply as much of a reflective, empathic, mistake-free environment as possible before allowing natural errors of empathy to occur. I wouldn't be surprised if Winnicott might see Kohut's first phase of analysis as a kind of unnaturalness that might not do the trick in his good enough terms. Of course, Winnicott always implied that a holding environment did have to be established before the patient could tolerate the disappointments, frustrations, regressions, and rages that can indwell the working out of the analyst's errors, but his process didn't seem to take the length of time of Kohut's carefully developed narcissistic transference. Perhaps one of the important differences here could also be accounted for by the fact that Kohut worked primarily with narcissistic character disorders, whereas Winnicott's patients were frequently borderline or psychotic. Also, it could be said that Winnicott was beginning to erode the concept of the exact interpretation and to turn failure into success years before Kohut brought his self psychology upon the psychoanalytic scene.

Several years ago I saw a male patient in his late twenties who complained of mild to moderate depression, a certain lack of goal direction, and a chronic sense of feeling empty. He had been in a long intensive psychoanalytic psychotherapy that seemed to have been pitched primarily at the oedipal level of development. This seemed justifiable, as the patient did have a neurotic diagnosis, and his major trauma occurred during the oedipal period when his father became ill. The therapy had been helpful, but the symptoms with which the patient presented tended to reemerge after the first treatment ended. The patient wanted to enter psychoanalysis because he felt that his difficulty must have had even deeper and earlier determinants than he had been made aware of during his psychotherapy.

One day toward the end of his first year of analysis, we were having what seemed to be an ordinary session. I had been up late the night before and was also developing the early symptoms of a viral illness. I fell asleep and dozed off for what was probably a few seconds. The patient at first started to talk through my little nap, but then gathered up the courage to confront me by asking whether the change in my breathing pattern was due to having fallen asleep. While my first tendency was to defend myself and give myself a chance to develop a strategy by asking the patient to associate to what he heard and felt, I decided to own up to the accusation and tell him about my missing sleep the night before and the feeling that I was coming down with something. After a moment of hesitation, he burst out crying. Once he could contain himself, he said that he was sure I would not tell him the truth and would try, as I had been tempted, to protect myself. He described his tears as those of gratefulness and closeness with me. He went on associating to the incident. Both of his parents had always tried to cover up their personal failures in a myriad of ways. It made him feel that he had to be perfect in order to gain their love. It was clear that the part of him that could have faults had to be buried and received no validation from his parents. He felt I had touched an area that had not been reached in his intensive psychotherapy. His first therapist did not acknowledge mistakes.

This rather significant failure on my part, my response to it and the patient's response to my response, became the focus of analytic work for some time. It became clearer than had been suggested during the earlier part of the year that the patient suffered from a true and false self disturbance and that there had been all too little validation of his authenticity during his early years. That issue was to become a crucial one in his analysis.

THE ACKNOWLEDGMENT OF FAILURE

This shows one way in which the therapist's failures as far as the patient is concerned, when dealt with in realistic yet tactful ways, can be turned around to further the therapeutic process. Winnicott tended to avoid the issue of whether and to what degree the therapist should acknowledge a failure. In his paper "Hate in the Countertransference" (1947), Winnicott emphasized the importance of the analyst acknowledging his or her capacity to hate the patient. Instances of hatred, according to Winnicott, occurred during every therapy or analysis. This hatred of the patient is universal, and during the everyday process of treatment, it is "latent," as he called it (dismissing a patient summarily, even though tactfully at a session's end, is a way the analyst's hatred is structured into the therapeutic situation). The therapist's hatred is both characterized by and paralleled by the mother's inevitable hatred of her baby, hatred that is, in both instances, handleable by the respective parties in the setting of a good enough holding environment. Winnicott (1947), in one of his most important contributions, stresses that it is necessary for the baby or the patient to experience hatred from the parent or the therapist in order to hate. He points out, "It seems to me doubtful whether a human child as he develops is capable of tolerating the full extent of his own hate in a sentimental environment. He needs hate to hate." (This sentence should do away with the unthinking claims that Winnicott was essentially a "momist.") He cites the nursery song "Rockabye Baby" to show the built-in outlets for aggression in motherhood.

Looking at the childhood model, it is easy to picture the mother, and father, sitting around with their adult offspring and their recent or not so recent mates, and reminiscing about how much ambivalence there had been during the tribulations of parenting. In good enough families the ex-children muse and generally forgive, and learn something. They are then a little more prepared to carry the process on into the next generation. Perhaps it is the model that led Winnicott to write this within his seismic paper on hate in the countertransference. Speaking of the analyst, he said, "Eventually, he ought to be able to tell his patient what he has been through on the patient's behalf, but an analysis may never get as far as this" (p. 198). He also wrote, "The analyst must be prepared to bear strain without expecting the patient to know anything about what he is doing, perhaps over a long period of time" (p. 198). While not meeting this issue in any detail, in another of his revolutionary papers, "The Use of an Object and Relating through Identifications" (1971e), very close to the end of his career and life, he wrote again of the analyst's failures: "Even this failure may have value if both analyst and patient acknowledge the failure."

My patient would not have been able to experience the re-creation of a failure unless I had validated his feeling that I had, if only momentarily, left him. If it had been an instance of a more direct personal aggression on my part against him, the same principle would hold. Winnicott wrote of the analyst's inner acknowledgment of his or her aggression against the patient at a time when he had not fully declared his independence from classical and Kleinian theory. He was also working on two important developmental and therapeutic issues, validation of the self by the object and the ability to internalize object usage through the interplay of therapist and patient aggression. These two developmental lines are inextricably interwoven. If Winnicott had continued his explorations, he would have had to acknowledge even more of his own aggression toward the patient by a more explicit permission to the student therapist to spell out therapist aggression when the setting is solid enough to handle it, and in a manner in which what is told to the patient is only that which is necessary for the occasion. Personal confessions beyond the need to validate the patient's aggressive impulses and implicitly reassure the patient that the analyst can tolerate his or her own aggression would only be an indulgence and an abuse, and not developmental usage of the patient.

HOLDING, HANDLING, AND OBJECT-RELATING

Winnicott's developmental lines of holding, handling, and object-relating can be applied to the therapy situation. Classically oriented therapists have done this intuitively by depending on their empathic capacities and their diagnostic impressions of the patient. However, there is a distinct advantage for the therapist when he or she knowingly applies this line to patients who require developmental "fixing" and who cannot become engaged in a meaningful, affective treatment relationship without first feeling well established and trusting in a stable, supporting, reliable setting.

Holding comes first. Winnicott (1962) saw that the issues involved were "in terms of motor and sensory elements. This would acquire a tendency towards a sense of existing." For Winnicott, the main task of holding the patient enables the infant to form a sense of continuity, *going-on-being,* as he put it so aptly. "All this tends towards the establishment of a unit self, but it cannot be over-emphasized that what happens at this very early stage depends on the ego-coverage given by the mother of the infant–mother coupling" (p. 60). The Winnicottian language and word linkage says something to the therapist. It is the therapist's job to find the metaphorical equivalence of the mother's basically nonverbal physical holding. This is a task of translation, from the nonverbal to the verbal. Winnicott referred to the issue in "Hate in the Countertransference" (1947): "For the neurotic the couch and warmth and comfort can be *symbolical* of the mother's love; for the psychotic it would be more true to say that these things *are* the analyst's physical expression of love. The couch *is* the analyst's lap or womb, and the warmth is the live warmth of the analyst's body. And so on"

(p. 199). Simply stated and conceptualized, but profound in its implications! Winnicott is of course referring to the developmental hierarchy of symbol formation. In out-patient treatment it is rare that the patient is so psychotic that the issue of physical holding comes into the mind of the caretaker–therapist. This work is more necessary during hospital care, where basic, "primitive" use of the symbolically equated (Grolnick and Lengyel 1978, Segal 1957) environment can be done. It is the work that was so admired by Winnicott, described by Madame Sechehaye in *Symbolic Realization* (1951). Sechehaye presented her food-refusing, psychotic young woman with pieces of apples, which were equated by the patient with the breast. The therapist did this while holding the patient and literally associating the breast and the apple pieces by their physical proximity. As the patient began to improve, the apples became "abstracted" into applesauce, which was eaten by the patient at a distance from the therapist. And words gradually became the substitutes for thing-apples.

In the out-patient situation, the sicker patients are usually not at a symbolic equation, symbiotic level, but more in keeping with that of presymbolic, transitional object and phenomena. In this sense the predominant transference is toward the therapist and the setting as a transitional object provision. So with the words of the therapist (Weich 1978). Studies have not been done, but it is likely that when the therapist is tuned into the right developmental station, his or her words would tend to have more textural, "thing," concrete qualities, and would deemphasize the discursive, presentational (rather than representational) aspect of language (Langer 1942). Presumably this therapist language would be more body language and imagistic to meet the patient's sensory motor and sensory tonic needs as well as his or her presymbolic needs. Hopefully the patient who is able to progress developmentally will build a fuller sense of and actuality of integration and continuity, the base for future self-evocable self and object constancy.

Handling is Winnicott's term for the more advanced phase of

physical interaction with the infant. This is the time of the gestural interplay that feels good to both parties. The environment is still necessary, for the patient's self-evocation is still in the future. This mixture of physical interaction and meaning in a setting of a good enough object relationship helps personalize the infant and develop what Winnicott termed the state of the "psyche indwelling in the soma" (Winnicott 1960d, p. 45). Winnicott uses the word *psyche* on purpose. He attempted to define it in his important paper "Mind and Its Relation to the Psyche-soma" (1949):

> I suppose that the word psyche here means the *imaginative elaboration of somatic parts, feelings and functions,* that is, of physical aliveness. We know that this imaginative elaboration is dependent on the existence and the healthy functioning of the brain, especially certain parts of it. The psyche is not, however, felt by the individual to be localized in the brain, or indeed to be localized anywhere. [p. 244]

Winnicott sees this stage of handling as an opportunity for the caretaker, whether parent or therapist, to establish this psychosomatic base that is *"felt by the individual* to form the core for the imaginative self."* A lack of an integration between the psyche and the soma could lead to a predisposition to psychosomatic illness and acting out behavior. Clearly with such disorders or patients with tendencies in this direction, the therapist is challenged by the need to meet with language and nonverbal gestural communication the needs of his or her therapeutic partner.

This handling phase merges seamlessly with object relating. It is here where Winnicott's concept of primary creativity comes into the picture. This phase essentially involves a parallel to the time when the infant waits for the mother to present a thing or a manipulation when the infant is ready for it to be there, creating the illusion that the infant created it (primary creativity). In his paper on ego integration Winnicott (1962) wrote, "In this way the baby comes to feel confident in being able to create objects and to create the actual world. The mother gives the baby a brief period in which omnipotence is a matter of experience" (p. 62).

How does this apply to the therapist? One way of looking at it is that psychosomatic play moves more into the early symbolic arena, actually the protosymbolic (Werner and Kaplan 1963). The therapist's words and acts become involved in the transitional process, enabling the patient to feel that he can create an object world that is not just projective or an extension of himself, but in part, the real world. (Gradually the object presenting therapist lends him- or herself to the patient's aggressions at both these objects and the presenter, thereby helping this created world to have an externality, a reality that can be used.) It is here that the therapist's creative capacities are most challenged. This is probably the same area that once was referred to within the classical analytic ethos as interpreting just a bit ahead of where the patient was, when the meaning was on the tip of the tongue of the patient's preconscious. But the difference here is that the therapist can use more than a discursive interpretation. Images, phrases, words even will do. And the setting and atmosphere must be one in which there is a partnership of play; when a meaning or word appears, the playing couple is not so dominated by one part, and it sometimes becomes unclear as to who set up a specific meaning or word. Thus, through the medium of optimal object presenting, the child is gradually induced into object relating.

A clinical example elucidates Winnicott's important developmental sequence.

Some years ago I treated a man in his early twenties. He can be called the Gardener, as his garden was virtually, or really, his whole life. He was short, slight, a little bit vacant in his eyes, and he spoke quietly and somewhat deliberately, without spontaneity. It turned out that his mother had insisted that he go to a psychiatrist because she had been concerned that after he returned from his job as a manager in a retail store, he spent all his time preoccupied with or working in his garden. He had no friends, had never dated, and showed no signs of being at all concerned about his mother's concerns. His mother especially, but also his father and other members of his family, frequently tried to pry him away from his beloved garden, but to no avail. He only felt more and more devoted to and concerned for its welfare. It turns out that the inspiration for the creation of what was a rather formal garden was the well-kept yet luxuriant garden of a woman whose house was along the route he walked every day from the bus stop to his own home. One day, while passing, he was so taken by the beauty of her garden that he resolved to duplicate it on his own property. It took several years, but he achieved an exact, almost mirror model of the other garden. At this point it became necessary to devote all his spare time to the mainte- nance of the garden. He treasured every hedge and every bud. He watched the buds for hours on end, and could almost see them grow into beautiful flowers. The Gardener especially esteemed his roses. In the evenings he would watch from his bedroom window, which over- looked the garden. If any of the neighborhood children or teenagers would disturb a hedge, or even a branch, during their episodes of horse- play, he would become extremely disturbed and rush down to chase them away. He would mourn over the loss of a carefully nurtured shrub, or even a twig.

The Gardener was willing to see me, at least manifestly, because he was afraid of his mother. There had been hints that she would destroy the garden unless he eventually began to move out into the "real" world. If the garden was no longer there, he would have no reason to live. Clearly his first transference to me was displaced from his mother. I was seen as her hired hand, someone who would eventually tread on his Elysian fields and destroy his paradise.

Fortunately for both of us, I had already become interested in Winnicott's concept of transitional object, and was able to see the garden as illusional, not delusional, and that it was serving as a transi- tional object that was bordering onto the fetishistic side of the spectrum. I knew I would have to respect the boundaries of his garden and of his ego, and that I would have to protect him from and differentiate myself from his angry and quite confounded mother. As the garden held him, it was necessary for me to hold simultaneously both him and his garden.

How was this done? By a combination of omission and commission. What was left out was any attempt to interpret the meaning, particularly the defensive or drive meaning, of my patient's use of the garden. As far as I was concerned, the garden was his entire life (even though it wasn't), and the adaptive and developmental illusion had to be maintained. For months we talked about his garden. I like gardening (to a degree) and think that if I had not, the shared illusion wouldn't have worked. I used whatever I knew and had felt about gardens and the plants they are peopled by. The Gardener and I shared our experiences and feelings about the mystery of how a bud becomes a flower, about the pain that occurs when the elements or careless humans harm any aspect of the symmetry of a garden, and about how there is something both thrilling and romantic about a rose and its fragrance that transcends other flowers. He taught me a lot about gardening and, surprisingly, I was able to inform him of a few things about which he hadn't been aware. In a sense, we talked of the birds, the bees, and the flowers, without talking about them. The symbol, or again, the protosymbol, was lived in without the disruptive and separating effects or bringing in the referent. We were talking of his love life and its vicissitudes. Love and the sharing of one's body with someone else is dangerous. It could break your limbs and your very self. He was frightened about castration and separation trauma. That was the symbolic meaning. But these symbols were only bits floating in a sea of presymbolic dangers and defenses. His garden was a transitional place in which and about which he could rest, gird himself, (fore) play, and practice a possible ultimate actual love life. Presumably his mother's hired hand surprised him by turning out to be with him and willing to be part of him and, because of my gardening sensibilities and knowledge, part of his garden. I was endowed with a transitional object significance that, before his therapy, had been exclusively invested in the garden. Even though his garden, the real one, was very much up front in reality, internally it had been hidden away deep inside of him. In the beginning the Gardener only humored me. It was only when enough time had been spent together in the garden that he allowed me to see this secret part of himself. This schizoid young man actually harbored deeply romantic emotions and desires to love and be loved. These desires could only be played out within the safe and comforting confines of his created garden, which had been constructed in the mirror image of the neighborhood woman's garden that he saw as an ideal. The garden had to be constructed from scratch to have had meaning. The woman had presented him with the images of the garden when he was ready to use them.

One may very well accuse me of building my own fantasy gardens of psychological plenty. Why was my stance toward the garden, which I would never have had the time or motivation to create myself, any different than, say, Alexander's manipulation of the transference? Wasn't I lying to the Gardener, deceiving him, and really contributing to his false self formation? No, but it is important to share some of the experience; it is crucial for an understanding of what Winnicottian therapy is. This patient's need for illusion and the need *not* to interpret defense, drive, and superego components of his symptomatology for some time were quite marked. But the principle can apply to many patients with various psychological developmental disorders.

My justification for the authenticity of the use of my "gardening self" is that the core of it felt natural. To some extent I had been there. Isn't it the essense of illusion that there is a core of reality around which it is built? This differentiates it from fantasy and delusion. The therapeutic arena is a theater, a place where illusions are allowed to become psychologically real. In the beginning the patient and I were only skirting his garden. He was suspicious that I was a "spy in the house of love," as Anaïs Nïn put it, and I was somewhat clumsily trying to enter into his experience enough to both *feel* and *be* authentic. But gradually a process began to develop between us and in the potential play space between us that allowed us to come closer and closer to each other's experience. He began to trust me more. And my counterpart experience was that I trusted him more. He became less of a pathological misfit and more of a romantic figure, even an artist. As he started to pick this up, he felt better about himself and safer to allow me further and further into his garden.

As this happened, my alter ego, alter gardener, role could relax a little, and to an extent he let me be myself. I could be more of the therapist, and I began slowly to express an interest in his past, an out-of-the-garden aspect of his life. He could begin to do this because he felt more secure with an ally, and he was starting to experience me more as a human being than as an inanimate object. What came out was most interesting.

His father had a hobby that involved the use of bundles of brightly colored wires. The patient was told that when he was an infant he had taken a piece of this wire as his security object. Then, when he was 4 or 5, his father built him a little go-cart that was constructed of wood and wire. He became attached to this cart for some time, and when it needed repair, his father would fix it for him. It became clear that the difficult relationship with his mother offered little solace and steadiness, and that he utilized his father and the objects he provided as developmental stabilizers.

The pattern continued into his adolescence. I was surprised when he revealed that he had become a scholar of bridges. A local suspension bridge with its delicate-looking yet strong vertical wires intrigued him. He went into the city's architectural archives to search out the original plans. In the back of his mind he was thinking of an article or even a book that he could write about the bridge. He would walk the bridge and savor its structural and architectural beauties.

During this phase of the therapy, which was always supported by journeys back to the garden, I felt we had moved from a holding to a handling level. We were having the equivalence of a gestural and action dialogue together. As with the holding phase, there was no attempt to interpret the symbolic, defensive, drive, or superego implications of this interesting developmental line that was emerging. It was material that I felt I had to contain, and contain myself from uttering any disrupting, clever interpretations. It was enough that he was aware we had moved into a new level of our relationship. The narrative continuity and the joint trip into the past deepened our experience together and provided an arena in which we could interchange ideas and clarify and share the various points in his life when he was affectively alive and, in a real sense, able to be in love, albeit the objects of his love had been first inanimate objects and then animate members of his beloved garden. By allowing a reexperiencing of his transitional worlds, I believed that a certain amount of loosening of development was occurring, allowing a furthering of both object relations and symbolization.

The tangible by-products of this process came in the form of his reports of a young woman he had met on a bus. At first they began to talk politely, then more conversationally. He did discuss his garden and found that it involved an interest that she shared. This new development (in both senses of the word) was another (pleasant) surprise to me. I had avoided, with difficulty at times, urging him to begin socializing. It seemed to emerge from him, and he felt it to be a change of his own making.

The Gardener's transformation continued as he began to report feelings of affection for the young woman. As might be expected, there was a concomitant but gradual waning of his preoccupation with his garden. The terms of endearment used for the roses and peonies were beginning to be applied to the young woman whom he started to date. The story was headed toward a happy ending when, after a number of months of seeing his partner and gradually having his first sexual experiences (without intercourse), of "neglecting" his garden, he announced that he was going to be engaged. This took place, and soon the two young people were married. They were able to successfully perform intercourse. The patient decided to stop his treatment at that point. Since it was only once-a-week psychotherapy, and a cognitive understanding in depth did not seem to be a real possibility at that time, we suspended our visits together after a reasonable period of termination. He never recontacted me, but later on I did hear that he had divorced after two years of marriage. Apparently there had been no reversion back to his garden.

A case seen so infrequently with limited follow-up is always difficult to evaluate. However, it is safe to say that there had been a developmental advance of a significant nature. The patient seemed to have had the developmental capacity to progress, within certain circumscribed limits, from Winnicott's phase of holding to handling to object relating. While there was a cognitive, insight element to the treatment, most of it was conducted with the insight in my head, not his. Without the psychoanalytic object relational understanding I had accumulated for some years, I could have easily become an antidevelopmental figure, forcing him more and more into his transitional-fetishistic world.

While this therapy is not ideal to illustrate Winnicottian therapy, it could be said that Winnicott's influence and ideas pervaded the interaction we had. The patient's regression to a kind of transitional object, protosymbolic level in his relationship to his garden, through the facilitating medium of the therapeutic alliance, allowed him to move closer to the truly object relational and the symbolic. That this was not a full move in those directions is clear. If circumstances had allowed, a longer and more frequent contact might have been more successful. But meaningful work had been done. If the patient's true self, his transitional object needs, his developmental timing, his protosymbolic use of language, and his need for a period of "going-on-being" had not been taken into account, the treatment would have floundered.

GOING IT (ALMOST) ALONE

One of Winnicott's most important contributions was his work on the capacity to be alone. This developmental line, which so involves our capacity to be reasonably mature adults, seems to have already been built into the therapeutic situation, even going back to Freud. In many ways the classical analytic situation consists of one person (the patient) working, free associating, playing (in a Winnicottian sense) on the couch in the presence of someone (the analyst) who sits behind the couch. How close this is to Winnicott's description of the baby's playing along but being supervised by a (hopefully) empathic caretaker who stays in the wings, available to move in when the contemporary capacity to go it alone is all used up and needs refueling! Clearly an analogy can be drawn between that developmental progression and some of the things that happen when a therapy works.

Although Freud obviously did not read Winnicott, speculatively he may have been tuned in to the same unconscious developmental issues. He placed himself so close, so very close, to the patient, but at the same time so far (out of sight). The patient led and talked freely, and the analyst was supposed to intervene only when the patient needed an assist to reach a degree of insight. I suspect that when there are developmental issues present in the patient in addition to conflictual ones, the analyst or therapist—as the case may be or calls for—consciously or unconsciously titrates his or her interventions in keeping with the patient's developmental abilities at the time, the capacity to be alone being one of these. The interpretations, or clarifications, or questions, may have, aside from their cognitive, symbolic meanings, the function of the analyst touching base when it seems appropriate to break the silence and provide a bridge. This intuitive, caretaking ability works also in the therapist's personal life, in raising children, in spouse relationships, in friendships.

Winnicott wrote about another aspect of this when he referred to the holding value of interpretations in an ego psychological paper he wrote somewhat early on, in the chapter "The Concept of Health Using Instinct Theory," included in *Human Nature* (Winnicott 1988):

> It can be noted here that the analysis of psychosis of schizoid type is essentially different from the analysis of psycho-neurosis, because the former requires of the analyst a toleration of actual regression to tolerate ideas and feelings (love, hate, ambivalence, etc.) and an understanding of processes, and also a wish to show understanding by appropriate exposition of language (interpretation of what the patient is just ready to allow to consciousness). A correct and well-timed interpretation in an analytic treatment gives a sense of being held physically that is more real (to the non-psychotic) than if a real holding or nursing had taken place. Understanding goes deeper and by understanding, shown by the use of language, the analyst holds physically in the past, that is, at the time of the need to be held, when love meant physical care and adaptation. [p. 61]

This is a statement that Winnicott respected the differences between treatment of the neurotic and of the more deeply disturbed. But characteristically he understood the similarities. Here Winnicott implies to the therapist that technique is adjusted to the developmental level of the patient and the limits of the therapist's understanding. When nonverbal needs must be met, too many words and too much meaning can preclude understanding. When higher-level, developmental internalizations have taken place in a good enough manner, the holding operation moves to the verbal, symbolic level. Whereas drive psychologists might have commented on this issue in their way by saying, "A good interpretation is a good feed," Winnicott would say it is a good *hold*. The important point is not to get caught in the dualistic trap of thinking that it is only the cognitive aspect of interpretation (with some affect thrown in) that changes the patient. This same thinking would claim that any theoretical or technical concept that includes the nonverbal and developmental is merely a "corrective emotional experience." In therapy and in life (which is more than therapy!), developmental progression occurs optimally when meaning and affect are as seamless as possible. When parents interpret the world to their offspring, if they do it with absent or inappropriate affect, the child is given disparate messages that don't fit immediately or ultimately insofar as development is concerned. The child is forced to imitate the limited communication or hide away his or her true communicative self deep within the psyche. It is self-evident that a developmentally tuned therapy or analysis must take these factors into account when there was affective-cognitive dissonance the first time around.

SQUIGGLING WITH ADULTS

Winnicott used his squiggle technique primarily in his time-limited consultations with children. He used it as a combined projective and therapeutic technique. Diagnosis and interpretations were overlapping and interwoven. But isn't this the way it is with modern theories of perception and meaning? Our observations and formu-

lation of the world are inextricably involved in constructed interpretations of the symbolic meaning of what we see. And when two
people are pursuing a developmental task together, the construction of the world (which allows reconstructions to be made later on)
is a joint enterprise involving a feedback communicative system. So
when Winnicott began to use his squiggle technique, he wasn't
really superimposing an artificial technique onto day-to-day experience. He merely epitomized that day-to-day experience in a
simple exercise that enabled him to engage in "simply one way of
getting into contact with the child" (Winnicott 1971d, p. 3).

A longer quote from Winnicott's introduction to *Therapeutic
Consultations in Child Psychiatry* (Winnicott 1971d) should help to
show the reader how he felt about and used the squiggle game:

> There is nothing original of course about the squiggle game and it
> would not be right for somebody to learn how to use the squiggle
> game and then to feel equipped to do what I call a therapeutic
> consultation. The squiggle game is simply one way of getting into
> contact with a child. What happens in the game and in the whole
> interview depends on the use made of the child's experience, in-
> cluding the material that presents itself. In order to use the mutual
> experience one must have in one's bones a theory of the emotional
> development of the child and of the relationship of the child to the
> environmental factors. In my case described here an artificial link is
> made between the squiggle and the psychotherapeutic consultation,
> and this arises out of the fact that from the drawings of the child and
> of the child and myself one can find one way of making the case
> come alive. It is almost as if the child, through the drawings, is
> alongside me, and to some extent taking part in describing the case,
> so that the reports of what the child and the therapist said tend to ring
> true. [p. 3]

A little further on Winnicott wrote that he gradually began to
realize that in these consultations he was in the role of the "subjective object, which rarely outlasts the first or first few interviews,"

but "the doctor has great opportunity for being in touch with the child" (p. 4).

The squiggle game can be thought of as a metaphor describing the essence of what is going on in Winnicottian therapy when it is working the way it works best. Winnicott is a subjective object to the patient, and the patient is a subjective object to Winnicott. In the quote above, Winnicott uses the phrase "as if," implying his conviction that a potential space between two subjective objects is set up in his kind of therapy (with his kinds of patients) and that it is probably only when this milieu exists that his contributions to psychodynamic technique can thrive.

Winnicott never directly advised a squiggling technique for adults. For the most part he kept it reigned into the limiting boundaries of the therapeutic consultation with the child. However, he always implied that it could be applicable to adults. Squiggling, bilateral mutual play, is at another realm of discourse than standard free associative technique. Squiggling verbally, interplaying the words and images of the therapist to construct a meaning between them immediately smacks of the impure, that is, the patient's responses are contaminated directly by the associations of the therapist. What kind of science is this? That's a hard one to answer— if the theoretician, or the reader, has a hard science view of the psychoanalytic situation, then the innovation may not do. However, with a more relativistic, hermeneutic, and dialogic view of treatment, squiggling might just be helpful. One could argue, after all, that the patient is so closely tuned to the person of and the expectations of the therapist that his associations are by definition always contaminated by the very presence of the influential therapist. So it could be claimed that there is an implied squiggling effect built into the very nature of psychoanalytic and psychotherapy situations. Why not make it explicit, and be able to take advantage of the benefits of the squiggling technique? What are these advantages? We can go back to the previous Winnicott quote, "The doctor has a great opportunity for being in touch with the child [substitute adult]." There are patients who cannot tolerate the deprivation involved in the classical technique of the plentiful patient free association and the rare therapist response. How many patients have called me in my capacity as a referral source for my hospital department and specifically asked, even begged, to have a therapist who will be active, who will provide feedback, who will be there! This kind of patient is better served by an interactive technique that insinuates itself into the derivatives of earlier developmental phases when reality was being constructed by both the parent and child. A relationship of a mature, internalized nature is not taken for granted, but *built* instead. To the extent that mutual meanings, understandings, and interpretations can arise from the treatment situation, the patient is provided with an externalized method of building a symbolic world that can ultimately be internalized. If this internalization does occur, presumably the therapist half of the squiggling becomes unnecessary.

Susan Deri (1984) wrote about the adult version of squiggling toward the very end of the last chapter of her book *Symbolism and Creativity*. The chapter is entitled "Fostering Good Symbolization." Referring to the need for what she termed "obsessive intellectualizers" to have a squiggling kind of experience, she wrote:

> Obsessive intellectualizers are in particular need of learning how to "play" freely and creatively within and outside of analysis. What they do not need is an impersonal, silent analyst who occasionally mutters "knowing" interpretations. This stance plays into their all-too-willing readiness to fill the role of "good patient." [p. 340]

A little later on she wrote:

> The patient's communicative and form-creative potential should be fostered by every intervention the analyst makes. Informative statements offered in a professional voice will not serve this aim. Only if interpretations are not "given" (in the sense of "pronounced"), but casually tossed into the patient's play space, i.e., into the transitional

space between the patient and analyst, only then can the patient pick up the offered material and weld it with his or her own inner content into a newly created gestalt. Put slightly differently: When the analyst's ideas are unobtrusively thrown into the patient's transitional play space, these ideas can lie around until the patient is ready to "find" them and blend them with his or her wishes and fantasies into a new, very personal ("treasured") possession. [p. 341]

In a footnote to this passage, Deri saw this process on a more abstract level as similar to Piaget's ideas of how new ideas are assimilated into new schema formation. Deri emphasized how the developmental use of Winnicott's potential space can foster the acquisition of higher levels of symbolization. She understood the need for some patients to be able to externalize early levels of more primitive, protosymbolic forms into a jointly built potential space in order to ultimately reach higher, more autonomous levels of symbolic functioning. While she stressed the obsessive intellectualizer, her comments apply to a wider range of "presymbolic disorders," which includes patients with significant developmental difficulty as well as many, or possibly most, borderline patients.

By now the reader must be crying out for a clearer way of understanding what might be called the dialogic squiggle. Deri was on target when she wrote of an interpretation "not being 'given' [in the sense of pronounced], but actually tossed into the patient's play space." When I am "squiggling" with adult patients, I feel that the patient and I are involved in a light form of Ping-Pong. Most of it consists of visual images that are evoked in each "partner," although these may be words or phrases that do not necessarily evoke strong visual images. The joint enterprise results in what is not too different from Freud's well-known comparison of the dream with the rebus, where the whole is constructed of combinations of visual and verbal images. Again, the difference between this and a more classical technique is that here the therapist decides that the patient needs another half and there is more to be gained from bringing in the "contaminant" of the therapist's projections than leaving the patient to his or her own devices. This occurs when the creative act of free associating is not possible and only occasional interpretive responses from the therapist do defiance to the patient's partially internalized object constancy.

A clinical example will help.

A while back I saw a woman in her early sixties who came to treatment for the first time after finding herself crying profusely during a Schubert lieder concert. The flow seemed to arise out of nowhere. She could only recall that it began during the last song of the cycle, "The Organ Grinder." She related the story and imagery of the song. The scene is winter and the wind is blowing. An old man dressed virtually in rags is playing his barrel organ in the street, surrounded by laughing children and barking dogs who are nipping at his feet. For no conscious reason the image evoked a profound sadness and its accompanying tears.

During the next few weeks the patient's story began to unfold. She was a book editor who thrived on reading and music. A long marriage to a dominating, apparently paranoid lawyer had produced no children. In fact, she maintained that all during her childbearing years they had not talked about having children. He never led, and she never asked. She related how an early difficult sexual encounter initiated her husband's refusal to have intercourse or engage in affectionate behavior of any kind. In public they were an ideal couple, attending parties and cultural functions. But at night he would lie in the bed with his back to her and she would have to be content with touching his back or arm. It became clear that she was a cyclothymic, passive, and masochistic woman who had developed a kind of folie à deux with her paranoid husband. Apparently it took a gradual accumulation of repressed rage and mourning plus the external stimulus of the lieder to bring her affects to the surface. Dialogue had broken down years before, and clearly had never been established in her original family.

In fact, it could be said that she was a master of monologue. After she told me her basic story in response to my questions, she filled the twice-weekly therapy sessions with ceaseless anecdotal accounts of her work life and her day-to-day experiences and frustrations. She seemed content to use me as a container and a holder, so great was her frustration and deprivation. When I thought the relationship was well established, I began to engage her in a kind of banter and wordplay that she was quite good at and enjoyed. She was a master of the verbal pun and used her wide cultural knowledge to "play" with me during these what might be called sessions in a rather sophisticated kindergarten. The foundations of a dialogue were being established. I began to feel that interpretive work was more of a possibility. In the beginning it had only served to break the continuity of our relationship and interfere with the holding environment she needed to provide a bridge from her pathological relationship to our therapeutic alliance. But I felt we had moved up the developmental scale in both our basic relationship and communication.

One session she alluded to her relationship with her husband with hints of an increasing sense of frustration and annoyance. I reminded her of the image of the organ grinder that had been so important in her decision to enter into an alternative interpersonal world, that of therapy. She countered my reminder by attending to the strength of the image of the barking dogs. She called them hounds. Francis Thompson's poem "The Hound of Heaven" came to my mind, and I told her that, in a bit of an ironic tone. She said that as soon as I said "Hound of Heaven," she saw the image of Cerberus, the three-headed dog who guarded the gates of Hades. She was then able to carry it alone. She had been living in a hell with her husband. Standing guard, like a dog, in fact, she was treated like a dog, at his master's feet. She asked how could she have done it all those years? She began to feel she understood how the deep sadness was able to arise during the concert. She saw how she was the beggar, looking for crumbs from her withholding and biting, sadistic husband. It was a breakthrough, not to deep layers of the unconscious, but a look behind the crumbling of some of the walls of denial that had characterized her life.

Sessions like this gave the patient the sense she had arrived at the knowledge herself, that it hadn't been superimposed on her by a dominating, moralistic therapist who would have been another version of her husband. But clearly, some of the work (or play) had been contributed by me. A more traditional therapy would have relied on her too much, a holding environment might not have been established, and the absence of a safe and secure environment for dialogic playing would not have allowed the kind of mutually arrived at meaning that was ultimately able to win out over her long-standing blindness. It could be argued that other techniques and theoretical orientations could have accomplished the same task. However, all too often this kind of patient is thought of as "untreatable" and that "therapeutic" maneuvers too early could intensify primitive defenses rather than help the patient to give them up.

Another clinical example might also be illustrative.

A bright and talented female teacher had a long history of early developmental traumata and resultant sadomasochistic fantasies. In one session she described one of these embarrassing fantasies, part of which consisted of a pair of lips facing a pair of vaginal labia, within a rather sinister setting. Almost immediately, I translated her image into my own, a Norman Rockwell Saturday Evening Post painting of an adolescent couple in a candy store, facing each other while sipping soda from two straws placed in the same glass. My image led her back to images from her past that involved a paternal aunt with whom she had a close relationship, quite in contrast with the stormy times she had with her often cruel, unempathic, and "gaslighting" mother. She recalled the close feelings she had when she played simple card games with her aunt. And she cried. The interaction between us had helped her to begin to see the sadomasochistic fantasies in a better perspective, not as shameful parts of herself but as products of a very difficult time during her early years. As with the first patient, the "squiggling" helped her construct a new meaning that she began to carry on herself with her own associations.

The question "What went on in these two instances?" must be asked at this point. How much were my "lightly tossed out" images, the Hound of Heaven and the Norman Rockwell cover, principally countertransferential projections and how much were they empathic responses to the patient's imagery and fantasies? No definite answer to this question is possible. The principle that therapist imagery and fantasies can tell us something about what is happening in the patient's psyche has been established in both the ego psychological (Arlow 1969) and Kleinian (Segal 1975) camps (in the latter in the form of projective identification). The radical nature of the squiggling technique is that it involves the sharing of reactive imagery in order to foster the associative and symbol building capacities. This technique has more advantages than disadvantages. An important example of a disadvantage is the danger of leading the patient—certainly a real danger. It is here that the therapist's own training and treatment come in, at least insofar as they offer the possibility of more perception than projection. However, even with optimal and long treatment and training, we are still symbolic animals; therapist meaning must have to intermingle with patient meaning. Since Ping-Pong is a fast game, there isn't much time for the therapist's ego-observing faculties to look over his or her intuitive-empathic response—for a moment, perhaps, but hardly more. It is here that the nature and qualities of the relationship come in. If it is one of hard-earned mutual trust and ease, the patient can serve as a co-guardian against the danger of having a pure projection inflicted on him or her. When the therapist's response is way off, the patient can, and often will, spell this right out, or, in his or her own way, drop it. If there is enough of the patient in the therapist's repsonse, if the therapist–patient milieu is right, then the patient can take up and use the therapist's contribution. Of course, this whole process involves a Winnicottian democratization of the therapy process that embodies his having analogized the "analyzing couple" to the "nursing couple." But so be it. There are problems with democracy, but most of us prefer it to totalitarianism.

WINNICOTTIAN CHILD THERAPY AND ANALYSIS

In a book that is primarily devoted to a Winnicottian view of adult therapy and analysis, the treatment of children, which he did so much of, has been given short shrift. However, with Winnicott, adult and child therapy were never very far apart.

The principal point is that there are some basic differences (as well as overlappings) between the use of play in Winnicottian child therapy and what we could call Anna Freudian, or certainly Kleinian treatment. It might be easiest to take Klein as the most extreme example. Klein (1932) used play as a substitute for the free association of adults. It was seen as a *means* of discovering the derivatives of unconscious symbolism. For Winnicott, when development was still possible, play was therapy in itself. It could be said that his play was situated somewhere between being and doing, between meaning and development, and, certainly, between reality and fantasy (Grolnick et al. 1978). When therapy is working optimally, these "betweens" become seamless, and the sharing of meaning, or the interpretive aspect of therapy, and playing a developmental partner become inseparable. By using play as such a central structure in his theoretical and technical contributions, Winnicott began to substitute the importance of bringing development and insight together in contrast to the more classical psychoanalytic emphasis on the combining of insight and affect. It is implied that playing must have its affective side in order to be playing.

Of course, this use of play as therapy is directly involved in Winnicott's way of doing adult therapy and analysis. However, the play enters the therapy session as more metaphoric and imagistic. Whereas any psychoanalytically oriented therapist would agree that in treatment at the symbolic level, affect and insight must go together, bringing in playing helps to counter the dualistic tendencies in psychoanalytic theorizing and technique.

Although children and adults are generally at different levels of development, it is clear from our patients and from ourselves how much overlap there is. Winnicott deeply believed that development proceeded throughout life, as did the possibility of creative living. Play, therefore, is a necessary part of living and therapy in both adults and children.

A "how to do it" stance both applies to and does not apply to Winnicott. I have been caught between the Scylla and Charybdis of telling the reader what to do, and presenting both Winnicott and myself as facilitators rather than dictators. But the "natural," talented therapist is a rare entity. The Winnicott literature should serve as a facilitator and "permitter" to allow the natural talent of the therapist to emerge. But this aspect of learning how to do Winnicottian therapy stirs up my superego concerns, some of them stemming from my own classical psychoanalytic training.

There is much about Winnicott that is reminiscent of the existential philosophers and psychologists. Ticho (1974) showed how the ideas of Martin Buber and Winnicott are similar, neither of whom having been directly aware of the works of the other. Buber's concepts of I-thou versus I-it and "seeming" experience are very close to Winnicott's true and false self concept. To both, to a significant degree the self is constituted by the other. One can mine such existential phenomenologists as Merleau-Ponty (1968) for similar compatibilities. The awareness of the existential aspects of Winnicott's ideas is a cause of concern among some psychoanalysts. The '50s—under the influence of the works of Sartre, Binswinger, May, and others—produced an existential analysis and therapy that was highly interpersonal, action oriented, intuitive, and anti-intellectual. While it took into account ideas beyond awareness, Sartre's (1953) unconscious was more like the Freudian preconscious. But Winnicott had a background of orthodox psychoanalytic training; a belief in classical analysis for the psychoneurotic patient; a developmental, historical perspective; a concept of internal, unconscious object relations; conscious and unconscious primitive affects; and even a continued utilization of the drive concept. The danger exists that his existential side will lead to an interpersonal, watered-down version of psychoanalysis. However, it is necessary to remember that in order even to get close to what Winnicott brought to his patients, a rather extensive knowledge of psychoanalytic theory and history and one's own personal therapy or analysis are essential. In other words, a Freudian informed knowledge of the basics of psychoanalysis and developmental theory, years of practicing and being supervised, along with the acquisition of a deep understanding of Winnicott's sometimes complex ideas, should help to ensure that therapy based on them will not degenerate either into wild analysis or nonanalysis, and will allow them to promote an important new addition to psychoanalytic theory and technique.

10

Caveats
for the Therapist

Now that we have seen some of the ways Winnicott's rich treasure trove of observational and developmental findings can be applied to the clinical situation, some caveats are in order. The same factors built into Winnicott's developmental system that could serve as pitfalls for a beginning (or not so beginning) therapist have provided fodder for his critics. Because of Winnicott's emphasis on authenticity, on the dangers of domination of the self by the internal superego, a controlling caretaker, family, educational or political system, it is not hard to view him as a kind of upstart, permissive, and self-indulgent type. However, these criticisms miss the point. The dialectic *between* freedom and conformity, *between* tradition and innovation, *between* authenticity and the importunings of civilization, and *between* gratification and frustration is the area Winnicott mapped out in which to study and work. It is how the polarities are distributed, and apportioned within these interacting systems, both within moment-to-moment living and throughout the life cycle, that Winnicott is calling to our attention.

Winnicott struggled himself with his *own* polarities. He spoke frequently of how, as a young analyst, he derived his satisfaction by making "smart" interpretations to the patient before the patient thought of them. Then when he realized the potential damage to the patient's sense of creative selfhood, later on he began to feel proud when his restraint allowed his patient to arrive at the interpretation. It might be added that, pragmatically, most of the interpretive work in a therapy or analysis derived from Winnicottian ideas represents a *joint* effort on both parties in the "analyzing couple."

With these general statements having been made, it is time to delve further into some of the specific dangers that could await the therapist who too avidly attempts to apply Winicott's appealing system. Spelling out these dangers presents us with another paradox: How can a therapist who is expected to be only good enough and who has to respect his or her own creativity and allow a field that permits trial and error do so when there are dangers of stepping on a mine if one ventures outside the therapeutic trenches? By no means can this seeming contradiction be passed off easily. But the model of the good enough Winnicottian caretaker can help us here. Therapy cannot and does not transcend life. We live with day-to-day dangers and ultimate dangers, death being the most serious of all. The parent who is preoccupied with the fear of life-threatening illness, electrocutions by open sockets in the house, or knifings during altercations in the schoolyard may all too easily overprotect the child. We all have to maintain healthy illusions that we are (basically) safe and that we can go on as if we live forever, *knowing full well* at the same time that this isn't so. It is this capacity for illusion, for the willful suspension of disbelief, that is most helpful in the therapist. It helps to create a safe enough field to work in, and yet, as with the parent, the therapist knows the countertransference dangers that lie ahead at any point. In fact, it can be said that one can't be a (good) therapist unless these dangers are well known and one can still be able to proceed as if they don't exist. So, with these qualifications and reassurances, let us move on.

CONCRETIZING WINNICOTT

One of the greatest sources of danger and misunderstanding is Winnicott's having bravely presented classical psychoanalysis with an alternative to Freud's structural model. For patients with developmental difficulties, the Winnicottian therapeutic situation offered a new developmental field and, by implication, a new developmental figure in which to attempt to repair the original damage by building new or collateral psychic structures. He stressed the presence of and the need for a degree of structural (not just topographical) regression in order for the original relationships to be played out in the transference situation. As has been explained in Chapters 5 and 6, Winnicott has traced out an important line of the ultimate development of mature symbols. Patients with significant developmental disturbance can have impairments in their capacity for a richness of symbolic thinking. Transferences with these patients are at a more primitive level, with the terms *symbiotic transference* and *transitional object transference* having been used by some. These transferences contrast with a classical transference, which is basically symbolic in nature. The therapist is a *symbolic* figure who represents past imagoes in the patient's life. The patient is aware of the "as if-ness" of the transference situation.

The problem lies within the treatment of the more regresseed patients. They require a supportive situation, more specifically, a Winnicottian holding environment. The model is based on maternal literal and figurative holding of the nonself-supportable infant. Therapists can be tempted to support suffering patients with some form of physical contact. In his later years Winnicott (1969) described how he physically rocked a *severely* regressed patient who was otherwise inconsolable. He found that the rhythm that seemed to help corresponded to the patient's heart rate. He also referred to the remarkable inpatient work done with a mute schizophrenic patient by Madame Sechehaye (1951), which was reported in her book *Symbolic Realization*. As I have related, the therapist very appropriately held and fed an extremely primitive young woman, giving her "pre-symbolic" apples. Later on, with developmental advance, a more abstracted applesauce followed and then, via a displacement process, a variety of other foods. These extreme situations challenge any therapist, and innovation and flexibility are necessary. But for the average expected patient, the holding environment is metaphoric and is supplied by the total supportive, constant setting and by the therapeutic holding effects of language itself.

Again, it is obvious that even a very regressed adult is not an infant or a child, and there are always areas of development present that are at the adult level. It is a mistake to reify Winnicott's model. The parent/infant–child situation always lies in the background of a Winnicottian therapy, but as a *scientific model* that can be used to generate hypotheses that must be *applied* to the therapist–patient dyad and not as a directly translatable set of instructions.

POETIZING WINNICOTT

Winnicott, the playful quixotic figure, can obscure Winnicott the scientist, the doctor, the pediatrician. Winnicott's tendency to thrive on ambiguity and his ability to poetize some of his language contribute to the illusion of the therapeutic situation as an aesthetic communication between two completely equal partners. Winnicott's emphasis on authenticity, on being, on action, and on impacting reality are certainly existential on one level. But his therapy is not existential therapy—the unconscious life and the patient's past are very much involved, and the therapist is always maneuvering from a nonverbal toward a verbal, symbolic level. Transference and resistance are vital aspects of Winnicott's system, which would not be so in an existential therapy.

When a patient is in a phase when the preferable medium for communication is language play and "verbal squiggling" (see

Chapter 9), there is a danger that he or she can be treated as a literary text and not as a flesh-and-blood person. This criticism has also been leveled at Lacanian psychoanalysis, which stresses the language aspects of analysis and maintains that the unconscious is structured as a language. Unless the language used has "body" and is affectively tuned, a Winnicottian therapy could degenerate into a poetic exercise that is every bit as intellectualized and "false self" as a badly conducted, intellectualized classical psychoanalysis, the very phenomenon Winnicott tried to avoid.

The romantic, Rousseauistic qualities in Winnicott also lend themselves to the tendency to idealize the patient. Winnicott did stress the intrinsic natural creativity and psychosomatic authenticity within each of us. The metaphor of the therapist serving as a kind of Michelangelo, delivering the work of art from the rough-hewn chunk of marble, is a tempting one. And many patients have such a fantasy, that they are Galateas to the therapist's Pygmalion. The kernel of reality within these patients' fantasies makes the countertransference deciphering that much more difficult. If these patients are quite sick, if they do have an aesthetic side, and if they have represented lifelong empathic challenges to their caretakers and partners, if the fit with the therapist is right, the patient turns to the therapist for life-sustaining assistance. The therapist hears that he or she is the only one who ever came close to understanding the patient, and the therapist is quickly idealized. One of the problems is that these tend to be patients who can work with very few therapists, and if countertransference challenges can be mastered, they can be very long-term, or even lifetime patients. They are the kinds of patients that led one of Winnicott's co-workers, André Green, to comment that there is no such thing as an unanalyzable patient until all possible analysts have been tried.

This all adds up to another Winnicottian paradox. There is sometimes a reality to the fact you are the only one who can treat this patient, just as if the mother is the best one to mother the infant. Yet at the same time, if the patient looked long and hard enough, you could be replaceable. The therapy sometimes takes place within this paradox. If the therapist recognizes the paradoxical quality to the dilemma, there is a chance ultimately the patient will also. And that could be a therapeutic milestone.

EMULATING WINNICOTT

Winnicott wrote a fair amount about his cases and the kinds of interventions he made. He is intuitive, evocative, always interesting, and seems to have been granted the devotion of his patients. In *The Piggle*, the account of a several-week analytic encounter with a young girl, he shines as he does in the short, almost magical, diagnostic and therapeutic moves he makes as elaborated in the important book *Therapeutic Consultations in Child Psychiatry* (1971d). He emerges from the pages of his writings as the therapist (or mother–father) you wish you had, and even his failures seem to have measures of success. How can a student of Winnicott's work not identify with him?

While Winnicott might secretly have enjoyed this imitation, overtly he would have deplored it, because an unassimilated Winnicott within a therapist would be no more than another false self. He would have been proud of a follower who used Winnicottian principles to find the most authentic, knowledgeable, creative, and civilized therapeutic self of which that individual was capable.

There is another interesting twist here. Winnicott was not always Winnicott. He was in a continuous struggle with his varied and complex sides, and he used, as most of us do, his own work to help continue or even begin the missing parts of his own analysis. One of the issues he tussled with was to control and master his teachy and obsessive self. He wrote about it and acknowledged, for example, that he knew he was not with the patient when he found himself making long and discursive interpretations.

Winnicott recorded near-verbatim notes of the analytic treatment of a schizoid physician he had treated during the war and who had sought him out later on for what turned out to be a two-year analysis. The transcript, which was first published in 1972 (Giovacchini 1972) and released again as *Holding and Interpretation* (Winnicott 1986), tends to stress Winnicott's interventions, and the reader is left with the sense that the analyst was talky, and sometimes preachy and intellectualized. Here is a sample:

> You are hovering here between the idea of your relation to mother alone and your relation to father and mother as a triangle. If father is perfect, then there is nothing you can do except be perfect too, and then you and father are identified with each other. There is no clash. If on the other hand you are two human beings who are fond of mother, then there is a clash. I think you would have discovered this in your own family if it had not been for the fact that you have two daughters. A boy would have brought out this point of the rivalry between him and his father in relation to mother. [Winnicott 1986, p. 96]

It would be difficult to characterize this long interpretation (which is placed in quotes in the transcript) as Winnicottian. It makes sense and could have been perfectly appropriate within the context of that particular patient–therapist relationship., However, it sounds more like the average expected analyst talking, and I would go so far as to say that any imitators would not be speaking within the spirit of Winnicottian interpretation. Thus, Winnicott's (and all other analysts') interpretations must be interpreted and placed in the wider gestalt of his contributions and any specific treatment dyad that might be in the mind of the reader. The Winnicott transcript referred to is an important document, as it is a rare chance to see a close to verbatim report of an analysis, especially one from such an important analyst. But just as there was a discrepancy between some of Freud's theoretical writings and his sometimes very pragmatic and human interventions, there is a variable gap between Winnicott's theory and his reported practice.

It is in the work with children that the special qualities of his personality and the innovativeness of his way of conceptualizing and using the therapeutic field come to the fore. Extrapolating this *spirit* onto work with adult patients may be the best way to take advantage of the uniqueness of his contributions.

CONCERNING MOMISM

At this point, a discussion of the danger of turning a therapy influenced by Winnicott's ideas into a "momistic" experience for the patient may be redundant. However, it is a recurrent accusation against Winnicott, and therapists have fallen into this trap.

Winnicott saw pure gratification and support as saccharine and inauthentic. A Winnicottian "momism" would be a good enough mom, one who must follow gratification with natural failures. It is true that, as in a Kohut-oriented psychoanalysis, there is a period during Winnicottian-oriented treatment of patients with identity and narcissistic disorders when it becomes necessary for the therapist to mirror and reflect back what has been received. Winnicott dealt with this specifically in his evocative and helpful paper "The Mirror-role of Mother and Family in Child Development" (1971b). Here he describes a woman of striking appearance but who felt that she was never truly looked at by others. Winnicott explained, ". . . In a way this patient's whole analysis revolved round the 'being seen' for what she in fact is, at any one moment; and at times the being actually seen in a subtle way is for her the main thing in her treatment" (p. 115). The necessity for the validation of the self was a crucial Winnicottian working concept. Further thought, I believe, can lead one to see that Winnicott's work on the mirroring function (see Chapter 5) contrasts markedly with what we understand by "momism." Actually the word "momism" was coined by Philip Wylie in his notorious 1942 book *Generation of Vipers.* The *Dictionary of American Slang* (Wentworth and Flexner 1960) defines momism as "the social phenome-

non of widespread mother domination; matriarchism as an infor-
mal power structure supported by sentimentalism; popular mother
worship." By this definition, on all counts, momism and Winnicott
are incompatible! Winnicott deplored domination by anyone,
despised sentimentalism, which he saw as basically sadistic, and
stressed the necessity for gradual but inevitable disillusionment
from any early idealism of the mother. So, for therapists who are
susceptible to "momistic" tendencies, it may be best for them to
think of Winnicott as anti-momist.

TRAINING TO BE A WINNICOTTIAN

Winnicott emphasized that creative thinking requires a sense of
solidity that comes from a traditional base of knowledge. He applied
that to himself and felt that his traditional psychoanalytic training
served as a kind of launching pad for his ideas, which were once
considered to be avant garde. He thought a classical background
was necessary to utilize the technical innovations that seemed to
flow from his theoretical orientation.

Winnicott was basically right. Concomitantly, as with any of the
psychoanalytic innovators who moved away from what they
viewed as a restricting orthodoxy, in order to understand their ideas
it is important to know their intellectual histories. This is true, for
example, with such recent original contributors as Kohut, Kernberg, Schafer, and Gill. Any theoretician, once steeped in traditional
psychoanalysis, will forever be in a dialogue with it, even if his or
her ideas have strayed in another direction (see Chapter 2 insofar as
it concerns the struggle Winnicott had with the principles of both
Freud and Klein).

Of course not every therapist, especially at this moment in time,
can or will obtain arduous and lengthy psychoanalytic training.
However, a solid knowledge of Freudian theory and ego and developmental psychology should be acquired. Learning about object
relations theory through Klein, Fairbairn, Balint, and Guntrip is

vital. Being analyzed, taking courses, attending related lectures, and being in supervision cannot be dispensed with. But since there is no distinct, organized training group for Winnicottian ideas, the main source of knowledge about his method is still his published work. Winnicott interweaves his theories and techniques throughout his writings (see Chapter 8). These writings are taken from talks to psychoanalysts, psychiatrists, social workers, educators, and laymen. Each audience evoked in him a lot of the same ideas, but also some differences. Ultimately, all or most of his work should be read. And the texture and the profundity of Winnicott's ideas make each rereading an opportunity for new understanding, new integration, and, frequently, a new perspective on the subject at hand.

Winnicott dedicated *Playing and Reality* (1971c): "To my patients who have paid to teach me." In my experience, my best Winnicottian teachers were, yes, my patients. Patients are universally well schooled in Winnicott. If therapists can only keep their sensibilities open, listen, and be patient and wait until matters unfold, the patient will either lead them or correct them. I will never forget one of my first patients. He was an adolescent who had tyrannized his family members, controlled their comings and goings at home, and eventually threatened their lives, leading to a hospitalization for observation. At conferences he was diagnosed anywhere from a paranoid schizophrenic to a "bastard" by countertransferring staff and attendings. He certainly was a mixed diagnostic picture and would best be described as borderline. When I tried in my youthful zeal to interpret and to help, and moved too quickly, he would tell me that I was wrong and that I was rushing him. If I sensed and showed any degree of aggressive countertransference, he would scream that fact back to me. I didn't understand him and was being cruel to him. Eventually he was able to persuade me that by taking away his defenses or threatening even in the subtlest manner his personal space or belongings, I was taking away transitional object crutches, or more often, fetishistic object crutches he vitally needed. If he sensed that I might be the slightest bit annoyed when he called me two or three times a day, he tried to reassure me that if I could be there and reassure him by my words, eventually he would not have to call me between sessions. (He was accurate.) Sometimes his anger at me would be so loud that his screaming broke the sound barriers between my officemate's room and mine, and it even reached out into the waiting room. He was my persecutory object; that was most clear. But when I realized that he was "training me," that he was a "training (an) analyst," I began to value him highly. When I started to move into his world, I found I could openly acknowledge my negative countertransference. Then I would find that this relieved him, as it gave him a sense of validation that he had all too little of in the past. When I praised him for helping me to understand him, he beamed, sometimes inwardly, and sometimes outwardly. We both began to feel that we had been through the wars together and that we were becoming a working team. At any given time I was sure that a disinterested observer taking a cross section through one of our sessions would be quite sure we were *both* daffy. But we had the courage to push on, and many years of work led to his being able to reach a Ph.D. level and go on ultimately to lead what was a sometimes stormy but often pleasurable interpersonal world.

Any patient is a teacher if the therapist is willing to relinquish the reins and become a student. But always remember that the student is also the therapist (another Winnicottian paradox we are better off not challenging).

Thus, in conclusion, the best Winnicottian teacher is a patient. But you can't be truly teachable unless you have schooled yourself both in his ideas and the ideas that nursed him.

11

The Future
of Winnicottian
Therapy

The vicissitudes of shifts in psychoanalytic theory and practice make it no easy task even to attempt to predict the future fate of Winnicottian ideas. It would certainly be presumptuous to ask for any more than Freud predicted for himself, an ultimate merging of his own work with that of others within the sea of ideas of Western civilization. While Winnicott was not as comprehensive and rigorous a thinker as Freud, he did cover vast areas of human behavior, experience, and endeavor. His ideas have increasingly affected our view of early mother–child relationships and the effects of dysfunctions in early development on later development in psychological life. Of course, it was not Winnicott alone—he is only part of a worldwide reaction to some of the excesses of the more positivistic aspirations of classical psychoanalytic theory. Kohut, Schafer, Sandler, George Klein, Gill, Stolorow, Fairbairn, Guntrip, Lacan, Spence, and Stern are only a few of the more outspoken critics and creators of major modifications in psychoanalytic theory. However, Winnicott occupies a unique position in this group. At this writing, his name appears in the bibliographies of established journals as frequently as Kohut, Mahler, and sometimes even Freud. Winnicott was the Dr. Spock of England and has had much more popular influence than the others. At this time, many of his unpublished papers aimed at social workers, teachers, and lay audiences are becoming available in books that are receiving wide distribution.

This is an eclectic time in psychoanalysis. Rather than there being one predominant model for the psychoanalytic situation, or one comprehensive theory, the psychoanalytic literature seems to accept both implicitly and explicitly (Pine 1988) the fact that there are at least three major psychoanalytic approaches—classical or structural theory, object relations psychology, and self psychology. The average expected psychoanalyst and psychoanalytic therapist who is not dedicated to one particular model or is not a follower of one of the reactive theorists tends to use theory in a very pragmatic manner, modifying it according to the patient and the fine-tuning of the therapeutic relationship, basically picking and choosing the theory (for many, really, model) that most fits the current therapeutic situation. While it is clear that classical theory is connected with Sigmund and Anna Freud, Hartmann, and at present Brenner and Arlow, and the self psychology school is still strongly associated with Kohut, the object relations school, the "middle school" of British psychoanalysis, has never made claim to a true leader. However, more and more, as the Winnicott literature expands, as his language becomes part of both professional and lay discourse, it is Winnicott's name that emerges as, if not the leader, the most prominent, creative, and comprehensive of the members of the British middle school. The principal schools are now identified often as Freud, Kohut, and Winnicott.

As object relations theory reaches its zenith of popularity, it is Winnicott who is most connected with that approach by the therapist and lay world. Of course Mahler made crucial contributions to this body of knowledge; in contrast, her clinical papers, especially on adult analysis or therapy, were relatively few. Winnicott kept his clinical thrust virtually throughout all his writings. So it is relevant but also ironic that it is only posthumously that this charismatic, brilliant man has assumed the leadership of one of the important schools of modern psychoanalysis. This is one of the reasons that we can think of Winnicott as a major force influencing the direction current of psychoanalytic theory.

Within the past two decades, the psychoanalytic situation is seen less and less as an antiseptic place to treat and experimentally prove the validity of psychoanalysis and more and more as a setting or stage in which to play and work out a psychoanalysis between two participant observers. Winnicott's work has greatly reinforced this trend. What are some of the implications of this general shift in direction?

The analytic situation originally was seen by many as a closed system, that is, a closed energy system similar to that occurring in a chemical equation. Object relations theory and the dialogic nature of Winnicottian therapy including the relationship of the individual and his/her surround are an instance of a mode conceptualized along general system theory lines (Sutherland 1980, von Bertalanffy 1933). More and more, the "ghost in the machine" is personalized, and psychological issues are talked about in terms of inner and outer objects (really people). Winnicott tried to keep his language "person-close" and to avoid the scientific jargon that characterized a phase of ego psychology that had its halcyon days from the 1950s until the 1970s.

Actually, the deliberate attempts of the American ego psychologists to scientize the analytic language was best spelled out by Schafer (1976) in the course of his attempt to free analysis of the structural model and substitute an action language model. Schafer, however, attacked the nominal and the spatial, and felt that the healthy analysand would ultimately speak less impersonally, claiming the responsibility for his or her own physical and mental actions. He felt the patient would do so at the verbal level, using direct language that utilizes verbs and adverbs more than nouns and adjectives, the latter tending to reinforce the image of the mind as spatial, and hence more disclaimable. Schafer's original radical attempt to do away with the spatial model never caught on directly, although it has been an important influence for more than a decade. But the work of Winnicott that is based on the idea that one must *be* before one acts offers a model that is more in keeping with personal experience and clinical experience. We always experience ourselves *both* in action and in spatial terms, with various hierarchal transitions in between. The model of a theater is compatible with current theory and seems to stem naturally out of Winnicott's concept of potential space. Life lives in the space *between* the dialogue of our inner stages and actors and our actual participation as a character in the theater of reality. This concept has been present in our imaginative literature for centuries, reaching prominence in the Renaissance concept of the theater as a dream (Cope 1973, Grolnick 1982). In contemporary drama it was well portrayed in Edward Albee's play *Tiny Alice,* where a small model of a house reflected as well as influenced the events of the larger house in which it was situated.

Essentially, the developmental line of the formation of internal and external images of the self and the other and the interweaving developmental line of the transitional process seem to have captured the imagination of the community of therapists. Not infrequently the sophisticated reader recognizes the similarities between Winnicott's potential space, Coleridge's willful suspension of disbelief, and Keats's negative capability. We do think of ourselves as existing in space and impacting on animate and inanimate objects that exist in that space. And with reference to the clinical situation, the more concretism there is and the less the internalization of self and object representations has occurred, the more patients think of themselves and others in spatial terms.

Yes, there is an everyday, common-sense appeal to a spatial model whose very basis is interactive. But there is another appeal. Referring to Coleridge and Keats, those who note this similarity but who have not been familiar with developmental theory tend to dismiss the novelty of Winnicott's conceptualizations. However, Winnicott has laid out the developmental roots and the developmental line of the object relational aspects of the capacity to form illusion, play, and symbolization, including symbolic space, that is, he has added depth to the concept. Those who can see this seem to be appreciative of and influenced by his contributions, recognizing their conceptual uniqueness within the psychoanalytic body of knowledge and how they enhance our present and potential understanding of the creative process.

WINNICOTT AND LACAN

Although this is not the place to explore extensively the basic similarities and differences between the ideas of Winnicott and those of an even more controversial figure, Jacques Lacan, it is worthwhile to spend some time discussing a few current trends on the psychoanalytic scene involving the ideas of these two influential figures.

Lacan has been an *enfant terrible* for traditional ego psychology. His ideas are complex. But one of the principal sources of their energy lies in Lacan's intense conviction that German refugee-started and American-finished ego psychology was inimical to the original ideas of and spirit of Freud. To Lacan, American psychoanalysts—politically and personally conservative and inhibited (in part by their own analyses)—spoke for the defensive ego to such a degree that psychoanalysis as a radical, freeing, and id-contacting method somehow frittered away. The Lacanian movement characterized itself as a return to Freud. The Hartmann-Kris-Lowenstein-Anna Freud ego became a tyrant to Lacan who saw ego psychology as a movement that, personally and politically, helped to bind rather than liberate the analysand and the Freudian movement. In this respect, Lacan and Winnicott have certain common denominators. Winnicott also reacted against the model of the ego building, prime mover analyst, and he thrived on allowing earlier, regressive aspects of the patient's life and experience to enter the psychoanalytic situation. Winnicott's Rousseauistic, play-oriented schema represented his radical side. The Winnicottian psychological field was more politically democratic than that of traditional analysis.

However, Lacan's emphasis on the verbal aspects of psychoanalysis conceptualizing the unconscious structured as a language, his virtual dissolution of a structured self, his emphasis on seeing one's self in the love of the other, his stress on the name of the father as an organizing signifier as well as his particular brand of play (perhaps its Zen-like aspects leading to the possibility of the five-minute session being used as an interpretation in itself) show the difference between Winnicott and Lacan. The early developmental, preverbal, play emphases of Winnicott take the more primitive, the more impulsive, and, yes, the more creative aspects of the repressed and split-off aspects of the patient into account. Winnicott offers more of a developmental, observation-oriented overview of the personality and the psychoanalytic situation. Also, Winnicott offers the vehicle of play as therapy in itself and the model of the squiggle game as a constructivist, creative interpretive tool. His potential space and its overlap with the concepts of Coleridge and Yeats have been intriguing to the intellectual. In essence, Winnicott helped to link the creative, the environmental, the cultural in such a manner that he has become intellectually challenging not only to psychoanalysts, but to family therapists, anthropologists, philosophers, psycholinguists, and art and literary critics.

The Lacanian movement has peaked, and a Winnicottian movement has begun to take its place. Important factors have been Lacan's relatively recent death, the many splits that occurred within Lacan's institutional psychoanalysis, the lack of a real observation-oriented developmental base, and the tendency among Lacan's followers to promote identification with an eccentric, idiosyncratic leader. These have led to such excesses as the five-minute hour and a certain "anything goes" ethos amongst his epigone. From the theoretical side, Lacan's anachronistic emphasis on the verbal and the symbolic in the therapeutic scope of his method (somewhat similar to Schafer's emphasis on the "I" as a verbal agency) limited his theoretical and technical systems. And it can be maintained that the mainstream psychoanalytic movement never really embraced Lacan, although it did spend some time jousting with his ideas. Lacan was too quirky, perhaps too continental. In Winnicott's case, in spite of significant ambivalence, American psychoanalysis did enter into a meaningful dialogue with his ideas and has gradually incorporated a number of his concepts.

The increasing Winnicott literature, both within and without the psychoanalytic movement, the appearance of Winnicott in the core curriculum of psychoanalytic institutes, and the gradual replacement of Kleinian, then Lacanian, and now more and more Winnicottian orientation in South American institutes all evidence the increasing use that the psychoanalytic community has for the ideas of this creative English gentleman.

Sherry Turkle, the Boswell of the Lacanian movement, while reviewing published English translations of Lacan's seminars, remarked that one might think that American ego psychology had become so "philosophically sophisticated" that it no longer needed the intellectual prodding of Lacan's return to the id movement. However, Turkle notes, while the autonomous "self" of Hartmann is now gone, "Heinz Kohut puts forth a self whose optimism, realism, and ability to stand aside from conflict make it not dissimilar from the autonomous ego that Lacan took to task a quarter of a century ago." One could debate the observation about Kohut, but Turkle has a point. Whether Winnicott's critical position toward ego psychology, his object relations, and his play-oriented stances can serve a similar Lacanian-like critical position remains to be seen. His ideas are comprehensive enough, are more pragmatic than philosophical (as are some of Lacan's), and yet retain the thrust of the repressed and the *regressed;* when applied appropriately with a little zest and gusto, the spirit of liberationism that characterized the more radical aspects of Freud's contributions can be retained. Of course, these remarks are made within the context that no theoretician reigns supreme. As Hartmann once dominated the psychoanalytic bibliographies and now no longer does, so it will be that a major theoretician and integrator will replace Winnicott, and, as happens in intellectual history, take along with him or her the "best of Winnicott."

WINNICOTT AND READER
RESPONSE THEORY

While Winnicott's influence on literary criticism—specifically, reader-response theory—may seem peripheral, it is relevant enough to warrant a short discussion. During the same time that Winnicott's ideas were becoming more prominent in the world of therapy, literary criticism, in its post-structuralist and now post-modern era, has become increasingly interested in the complex interaction between the reader and the literary text. Some are more conservative, where there is only one interpretation to a text; it was in the author's conscious mind and it is the job of the critic to immerse himself or herself in the author's time and place so he or she has a chance of reproducing an authoritative interpretation (Hirsch 1967). The other side of the spectrum sees the text as the possession of the critic; in a radical, subjective hermeneutics, the critic has a right to appropriate the text in the context of his or her (the critic's) present time and place and do with it as he or she wants. Derrida (1974) can be used as an example of this school.

Essentially, one group is more objectivist and one more subjectivist. The extremist positions involved here were not resonant with the sensibilities of some psychoanalytic theorists. Murray Schwartz, a psychoanalytic critic, asks meaningfully, "Where is the text?" (Schwartz 1978). For Schwartz, the text is *between* the reader and the actual text. The antidote to a radical subjectivism is to maintain the illusion that the text is shaped by both the reader and the author. Norman Holland (1975) studied a number of readers reading and tried to show this constructivist approach in a near clinical manner.

It is not surprising that both Schwartz and Holland invoked Winnicott's concept of potential space to provide a theoretical base for their points of view. The transitional process, seen in mother–infant and therapist–patient dyads, can be invoked in the reader–text dialogic dyad. It does make sense. The squiggle game can provide a model for the complex interaction between the reader (or interpreter) and the text. Meaning is not just objectively *there* waiting to be archaeologically delivered. But can the text be seen as any potentially symbolic structure, to be bathed with meaning from the subjective world of the reader? Schwartz, Holland, Green, and others see the world of potential space, illusion, and mutual construction as more explanatory.

This has clear implication for the psychoanalytic and psychotherapeutic processes. The patient's statements can be seen in part as a text and the psychotherapist as a reader of that text and vice versa. This model has been a seductive one, as it has been presented by the literary world, and some psychoanalysts have been attracted to it (Schafer 1983, Spence 1982). This has resulted in a subjectivist school in psychoanalysis. The objectivists have been around a long time and are represented by the followers of the structural, conflict model, where insight and reconstruction still aim toward validity rather than mutually agreed-upon meaning. It is regarding the latter philosophical stance that Winnicott has offered to us a kind of compromise where the subjective and the objective work together within the transitional process. The dialectics within both theory building and intellectual history may be bringing us more and more in Winnicott's direction.

THE WIDENING SCOPE OF PSYCHOANALYSIS

Since the 1960s psychoanalysis has been stimulated and prodded by the concept of the "widening scope of psychoanalysis." It was Leo Stone (1954) who put the concept on the psychoanalytic map.

Psychoanalysis, no longer in its golden age when waiting lists of neurotic patients ran more than a year, was advised that there may be a population accessible to the method that had been excluded in the past. Perhaps certain patients with severe personality disorders, manifestations of perversions, and psychosomatic illness could be treated with classical psychoanalysis, using only occasional deviations from what was considered standard technique. Many of us felt that Stone and others within the widening scope movement were only spelling out and giving permission for a phenomenon that already was in place. Psychoanalysts were seeing sicker patients because these patients were presenting themselves more frequently than psychoneurotic patients, and theoretical justifications for making modifications were already beginning to appear in the literature. Winnicott, among others of course, was instrumental in beginning to provide this theoretical justification, and it is Winnicott's work that now and in the future will be pointing the way to a psychoanalysis that regards the treatment of these more disturbed patients as true psychoanalysis rather than a second class, modified form. By bringing in a new, more process, general system way of thinking and demonstrating its developmental roots in the early mother–child interaction, Winnicott has been gradually helping to legitimize the widening scope. I predict a day when the treatment of cases he had to call research cases will be considered as psychoanalytic as the treatment of the still sought-after verbal, internalized psychoneurotic patient who is treated with standard technique. This standard treatment presently still smacks of earlier attempts to see psychoanalysis as an experimental science and treatment, where the variables could be controlled clinically to such a degree that one could claim hard science events were occurring during the course of a psychoanalysis.

THE PHILOSOPHICAL BASE
OF WINNICOTTIAN THERAPY

A discussion of the fundamental philosophical difference between classical and Winnicottian therapy is in order at this point. Winnicottian therapy does share with classical psychoanalysis the concepts of the unconscious, transference, countertransference, resistance, some important elements of psychic determinism, and the importance of insight. However, there are differences.

It is ironic that the defining image of classical psychoanalysis has been to some extent an aspect of its external or behavioral dimensions. What is psychoanalysis? The educated responder would often tend, understandably, to define it by its location—the couch, its frequency (four or five times a week), the qualifications of its participants (a neurotic patient and a trained and analyzed analyst). The irony is that a process that involves the inner world—the study, understanding, and changing of the intrapsychic representations of the outer world—is defined so much by a standard that is descriptive and behavioral in its nature. This is also true, to a degree, within the training institutions of organized psychoanalysis.

Winnicott once answered the question "When is psychoanalysis taking place?" by saying, "It depends upon who's doing it." I believe that Winnicott thought of himself as a trained psychoanalyst who knew, lived, and breathed the psychoanalytic epistemology and ethos. He thought of himself as *doing* psychoanalysis, even when he was seeing a patient for one diagnostic-therapeutic visit (Winnicott 1971d). In keeping with an implicit, more act than content, psychology, Winnicott believed that the essence of psychoanalysis was thinking in psychoanalytic-interpretative terms. It is ideal when both patient and therapist are doing the same thing. But even in unmodified classical psychoanalysis for long periods of time during an analysis, the psychoanalyst, by definition, is running somewhat or very much ahead of the patient. The fact that these two unequal partners are in their psychoanalytic places (behind and on the couch) doesn't in itself ensure that psychoanalysis is taking place for so much of the time during the procedure. It is the continuous process of interpretation that is principally in the analyst's mind that defines it as psychoanalysis.

A Winnicott-oriented point of view here would say that an analyst who has put on his or her psychoanalytic thinking cap and is interpreting (whether silently or verbally) is doing psychoanalysis. One could extend this to say that if there is a patient present frequently, it is classical analysis; if it is a work of art or a social rite, it is applied psychoanalysis. Each of these psychoanalytic fields would have its own methodology, as would a single or several diagnostic-therapeutic interviews (Wurmser 1976).

This philosophical stance runs into potential difficulty because of the danger of looseness and the possibility that the grandiosity of being analytically trained, or even analytically oriented, would invite the therapist to think that whenever he or she thinks, psychoanalysis is taking place. (Of course, the mental set of psychoanalysis is a *special* state of mind and consciousness that must be invoked by the analyst.)

The advantage, however, of this act psychological view of analysis would be that psychoanalysis would be possible under a wider variety of situations. The method would not have to be stretched and modified, as it is now, in order to meet the psychiatric needs of the population and the economic needs of the therapist. The major criteria would be whether the psychoanalytic process was actively occurring in the mind of the therapist and whether that process was fundamentally geared toward enabling a similar process ultimately to occur in the mind of the patient.

Of course, seeing a borderline patient twice a week and thinking psychoanalytically, while holding off any uncovering interpretations, is far from the termination phase of a successful analysis where the patient's and the analyst's interpretative work are often interweaving, sometimes quietly and sometimes out loud. And one would have to acknowledge that the way the analyst of this borderline patient *works* is quite different than with the close-to-termination psychoanalytic patient. However, the essential point is that the *kind of thinking,* the kinds of issues, are *qualitatively* the same, whether held within the therapist, shared with the patient later on, overtly and summarily interpreted, or, when appropriate, doomed never to be uttered.

AN OVERVIEW

It is here that Winnicott's work, both explicitly and implicitly, makes a furthering contribution to psychoanalysis. Winnicott's emphasis on the dyads, patient–therapist and mother–child, and his equally important emphasis on the total psychoanalytic or therapeutic setting makes a powerful psychoanalytic statement. Before the object relations school and the self psychology school appeared, classical psychoanalysis saw the setting as a necessary condition for insuring the validity of and scientific status of psychoanalysis. The steadiness, the buffering effect, the holding effect, the containing effect, the steadying effect, its flexibility combined with a relative indestructability, were extratheoretical givens and seemed to be more epiphenomena of the therapy process and its necessary conditions than they were an intrinsic part of that process (this is perhaps an extreme statement, but it is still essentially valid).

With a fundamentally different theoretical view of the setting, and a philosphically different view of what a psychoanalytic process is, Winnicott's (and related) ideas have the possibility of influencing an ultimate change in the way we see psychoanalysis. If the process can be, at first, in the mind of the therapist, and at the same time be present in the here-and-now interplay between the therapist and patient; if presymbolic (or protosymbolic) disorders can be worked with psychoanalytically without having to think that a certain behaviorally determined set of rules is necessary for psychoanalysis to take place—then it is possible that psychoanalysis can be used with more and more diagnostic groups of patients. The concepts of modifications and parameters would not be used in the same sense they are now, and both the therapist and the patient would be able to work in a freer, more open, and, consequently, more creative field.

The work and theories of Lacan, Schafer, and Kohut, for example, have attempted to cut through the depersonalizing aspects of psychoanalytic structural theory. Clearly Lacan and Schafer have not been "bought" by American psychoanalysis. Kernberg has tried to use some of Winnicott's ideas (particularly the holding environment) in his complex theoretical structure, which includes elements of general object relations theory, drive theory, and ego psychology. To many, his contribution represents a noble attempt at combining existing theories; however, they seem to consist of an eclectic pasting together of various theories, leading to the necessity for somewhat rigid technical rules to hold the system together. As we begin to see the comprehensive nature of Winnicott's theoretical, descriptive, and technical systems and how close they are to each other, clinicians should find his ideas more and more useful.

It is necessary for clinicians to study Winnicott enough to realize that the curative process he advocates is far more complex than a reductionistic change through empathy or mother love, and that there is ample room for the conceptualization of insight and the use of aggressive drive or affect. In fact, Winnicott's developmental process doesn't work without healthy thrusts of developmental aggression. Necessary internalizations would not occur and the reality of the object and its use would be limited. Again, Winnicott saw the saccharine treatment of children and patients as destructive.

Thus Winnicott has left us with a rich developmental theory and an open-ended, creatively oriented palette of technique that can be both used and expanded upon. While no man or woman's work is ever the final answer, the increasing use of Winnicott in our therapy literature represents a realization that his system presently offers a refreshing creative middle ground between the sometimes clashing polarized schools that currently preoccupy the psychoanalytically oriented community.

Appendix:
A Winnicottian
Annotated
Bibliography

BOOKS RELATED TO WINNICOTT

Bachelard, G. (1938). *The Poetics of Space.* Boston: Beacon Press, 1969.

A fascinating study of the phenomenology of space by a philosopher and poet. Bachelard provides a mix of images about familiar, poetic space that meshes well with Winnicott's views of illusion and potential space. Well worth the read.

Bollas, C. (1987). *The Shadow of the Object.* New York: Columbia University Press.

This very sensitive, predominantly clinical study begins with Winnicott but decidedly ends with Bollas. He is one of the most original of the Winnicottians and has shown how one can use Winnicott to help find one's own ideas. It also helps that Bollas listens so carefully to his patients.

Clancier, A., and Kalmanovitch, J. (1984). *Winnicott and Paradox: From Birth to Creation.* London: Tavistock, 1987.

Basically, this is a paean to Winnicott by two of his followers. It is a helpful exposition of some of his ideas. It also includes reminiscences about Winnicott, the man, by some important figures in international psychoanalysis.

Davis, M., and Wallbridge, D., eds. (1981). *Boundary and Space: An Introduction to the Work of D. W. Winnicott.* New York: Brunner/ Mazel.

The first attempt to provide the reader with most of Winnicott's concepts. It is presided over by two members of the Winnicott Trust editorial board. For the most part it is not critical but explanatory. For a shortcut to Winnicott it is useful.

Deri, S. (1984). *Symbolization and Creativity.* New York: International Universities Press.

Deri's continental, clinical, and intellectual background as well as her artistic temperament helped her to truly understand what Winnicott had to say. She found her own way of using his ideas clinically, and her last book demonstrates this well.

Eigen, M. (1986). *The Psychotic Core.* Northvale, NJ: Jason Aronson.

A complex but rewarding book on psychotic processes, using a Winnicottian backdrop.

Fromm, M., and Smith, B., eds. (1989). *The Facilitating Environment: Clinical Applications of Winnicott's Theory.* Madison, CT: International Universities Press.

A large collection of papers clustered around the clinical implications of Winnicott's theory. Principally conceptualized by hospital-based therapists at the Austin Riggs Center. While a little uneven, as are most collections of this type, it is spirited and provocative.

Fuller, P. (1980). *Art and Psychoanalysis.* London: Writers and Readers Publishing Cooperative.

How an art critic can use ideas of Winnicott and Milner. An uneven but interesting book that is part of the trend that is moving from Lacan toward Winnicott.

Green, A. (1986). *On Private Madness.* London: The Hogarth Press and the Institute of Psycho-Analysis.

Green is one of France's most influential psychoanalytic and literary critics. He first followed Lacan, and then became influenced by Winnicott, serving as one of his most active advocates. Green's writings are continental in their form, but a little work on the part of the reader will invariably be most rewarding.

Gombrich, E. (1964). *Art and Illusion.* Princeton, NJ: Princeton University Press.

A view of the creative process and illusion from an important and astute art historian and critic. Gombrich and Langer help to give the psychoanalytic student of Winnicott and object relations theory a broader perspective.

Grolnick, S., Barkin, L., in collaboration with W. Muensterberger, eds. (1978). *Between Reality and Fantasy: Transitional Objects and Phenomena.* Northvale, NJ: Jason Aronson.

The first collection of papers on Winnicott concentrating on his concept of the transitional process. There are developmental, clinical, and applied papers, some of which are now basic.

Grosskurth, P. (1986). *Klein: Her Work and Her Life.* New York: Alfred A. Knopf.

A long, somewhat exhaustive, but nevertheless almost always interesting biography of Klein that gives just due to Clare and Donald Winnicott. Winnicott's future biographer should find Grosskurth a good source.

Holland, N. (1975). *Five Readers Reading.* New Haven, CT: Yale University Press.

A close to clinical exposition of Winnicottian-based view of literary criticism. The author is an important American literary critic who underwent psychoanalytic training.

Hughes, J. (1989). *Reshaping the Psychoanalytic Domain: The Work of Melanie Klein, W. R. D. Fairbairn, and D. W. Winnicott.* Berkeley: University of California Press.

A kind of primer by a historian on the evolution of the object relations school out of more classical analysis. The book can be of assistance, but could have been more inquisitive concerning the historical antecedents of the middle school.

Khan, M. (1974). *The Privacy of the Self.* New York: International Universities Press.

A sensitively written collection of papers by one of Winnicott's editors and closest followers.

Kuhns, R. (1983). *Psychoanalytic Theory of Art: A Philosophy of Art on Developmental Principles.* New York: Columbia University Press.

A sophisticated piece of aesthetic critical theory by a professor of philosophy at Columbia University. Kuhns finds Winnicott most useful, but does discuss other psychoanalytic theoreticians.

Langer, S. (1942). *Philosophy in a New Key.* Cambridge, MA: Harvard University Press.

A most important study by a philosopher of symbolism who was one of Ernst Cassirer's students. Langer sensitively discusses aesthetic symbols and provides a good background for understanding the differences between presentational and representational symbolism. She anachronistically helps the Winnicott student to understand the more advanced levels of his concepts of illusion and potential space as well as the ultimate fate of transitional language.

Meissner, W. (1984). *Psychoanalysis   and Religion.* New Haven, CT: Yale University Press.
An important book by a man who has combined the best of both his Jesuitism and psychoanalysis. Meissner helps to fight the historical reductionistic psychoanalytic attitude toward religion, using Winnicott along the way.

Milner, M. (1987). *The Suppressed Madness of Sane Men: Forty-four years of Exploring Psychoanalysis.*   London: Tavistock.
Milner was one of Winnicott's most simpatico co-workers. This collection of her Winnicott-influenced papers is written from the clinical, theoretical, aesthetic standpoint. She is particularly good in helping to spell out a broader psychoanalytic theory of symbolism.

Modell, A. (1968). *Object Love and Reality: An Introduction to a Psychoanalytic Theory of Object Relations.* New York: International Universities Press.
An "early" American exposition of object relations theory by a continued advocate of some of Winnicott's theoretical positions. It includes one of the first attempts to apply Winnicott to art, in this case prehistoric art.

Ogden, T. (1986) *The Matrix of the Mind: Object Relations and the Psychoanalytic Dialogue.* Northvale, NJ: Jason Aronson.
An up-to-date study on object relations with due attention to Winnicott.

Phillips, A. (1988). *Winnicott.* London: Fontana Press. Also published by Harvard University Press.
An erudite, thoughtful, close reading and critique of Winnicott's ideas. The kind of work that appreciates and respects Winnicott's status as a psychoanalytic intellectual.

Rizzuto, A. (1981). *The Birth of the Living God: A Psychoanalytic Study.* Chicago: University of Chicago Press.

An fascinating, Winnicott-influenced but original view of religious experience by a well-informed female psychoanalyst. It is both clinical and theoretical, and well worth owning.

Rodman, F., ed. (1987). *The Spontaneous Gesture: Selected Letters of D. W. Winnicott.* Cambridge, MA: Harvard University Press.

An interesting, stimulating collection of Winnicott's letters with a sensitive and helpful introduction by the editor.

Searles, H. (1960). *The Non-Human Environment.* New York: International Universities Press.

A solid and elucidating view, highly influenced by Winnicott, of our relationship to the nonhuman environment.

ARTICLES RELATED TO WINNICOTT

Beres, D. (1960). Symbol and object. *Bulletin of the Menninger Clinic* 29:2–23.

Beres is a savvy, broad-thinking ego psychologist who recognized the limits of a conflict model of symbol formation. This paper shows the kind of progressive thinking involved in his contributions.

Gaddini, R. (1970). Transitional objects and the process of individuation: a study in three different social groups. *Journal of the American Academy of Child Psychiatry* 9:347–364.

An important research study carried out in modern Rome in which it was shown that sleeping arrangements are crucial in determining the potential development of a transitional object.

Greenacre, P. (1969). The fetish and the transitional object. *Psychoanalytic Study of the Child* 24:144–164. New York: International Universities Press.

_____ (1970). The transitional object and the fetish with special reference to the role of illusion. *International Journal of Psycho-Analysis* 51:442–456.
Two basic papers from an early backer of Winnicott's ideas. Greenacre uses her extensive clinical and theoretical background to discuss the transitional object concept in relation to fetishism and creativity.

Grolnick, S. (1984). Play, myth, theater and psychoanalysis. *The Psychoanalytic Review* 71:247–262.
A paper that attempts to give a historical, mythological, and theatrical perspective on Freudian and Winnicottian treatment, showing how much a dramatistic model is built into Winnicott's method of treatment.

Grolnick, S., and Grolnick, M. (1981). The Little Lame Prince. *The Psychoanalytic Study of Society* 9:161–180.
A critical study using Winnicottian theory of a nineteenth-century children's story in the form of a fairy tale. The issue of when transitional objects first appeared historically in Western society is discussed.

Guntrip, H. (1975). My experience of analysis with Fairbairn and Winnicott. *International Review of Psycho-Analysis* 2:145–156.
This paper is now a near classic in the Winnicottian literature. Guntrip contrasts Fairbairn's more formal analyzing style with Winnicott's. For those who want a good feeling of the middle school, this is a must.

Kafka, J. (1969). The body as transitional object: a psychoanalytic study of a self-mutilating patient. *British Journal of Medical Psychology* 42:207–212.
Kafka writes about an intriguing treatment that involved the complex issue of the body as a transitional object. It is a very useful paper, particularly in the treatment of borderline patients.

Kahne, M. (1967). On the persistence of transitional phenomena into adult life. *International Journal of Psycho-Analysis* 48:247–258.

One of the earliest attempts to tease out a life-span theory from Winnicott's work. It can serve as an evocative stimulus to observation and thinking about this area.

Lindner, S. (1879). The sucking of the fingers, lips, etc. by children (pleasure sucking). *Storia e Critica Della Psicologia* 1:111–143, 1980.

An interesting piece of security object history with an introduction by M. B. Macmillan. Lindner was a pediatrician who described the use of what were mostly fetishistic security objects. The paper's interest and value are enhanced by the graphic illustrations. In English.

Little, M. (1985). Winnicott working in areas where psychotic anxieties predominate: a personal record. *Free Associations* 3:9–42. London: Free Association Books.

A highly personal account of Little's third treatment, an analysis with Winnicott. It is invaluable for those interested in just how Winnicott worked.

McDonald, M. (1970). Transitional tunes and musical development. *Psychoanalytic Study of the Child* 25:503–520. New York: International Universities Press.

An early Winnicottian-influenced paper that shows how music can develop into transitional phenomena. McDonald also presents an interesting discussion of the Suzuki method of teaching very young children how to play the violin.

Muensterberger, W. (1962). The creative process: its relation to object loss and fetishism. *The Psychoanalytic Study of Society* 2:161–185.

A highly original paper that has become a classic in this area. Muensterberger uses his combined psychoanalytic and anthropological training in a cross-cultural study of the complex relationships between the transitional object, fetishism, art, and object loss.

Pedder, J. (1977). The role of space and location in psychoanalytic therapy, play, and theater. *International Review of Psycho-Analysis* 4:215–224.

A fine exposition of the dramatistic model that is built into Winnicott's theories.

Rosen, V. (1964). Some aspects of artistic talent on character style. *Psychoanalytic Quarterly* 33:1–23. Collected in *Style, Character and Language,* ed. S. Atkin and M. Jucovy, pp. 331–352. New York: Jason Aronson, 1976.

Rosen was one of ego psychology's intellectual giants. Here he shows his clinical acumen by demonstrating how an experience in childhood with a crucial transitional object appears in adulthood within character style. The paper has rather profound implications.

Schwartz, M. (1978). Critic, define thyself. In *Psychoanalysis and the Question of the Text,* ed. G. Hartman. Baltimore: The Johns Hopkins University Press.

Schwartz, a colleague of Norman Holland, uses Winnicottian-influenced ideas to discuss the subject–object controversy in postmodern literary criticism. He opts for seeing the text as existing *between* the reader and the actual narrative text.

Sperling, M. (1963). Fetishism in children. *Psychoanalytic Quarterly* 32:374–393.

A view from the other side. Sperling was convinced, in decided contrast with Winnicott and Greenacre, that the presence of a transitional object in childhood was a sign of a pathological mother–child relationship. Later on Sylvia Brody carried on some of the same point of view, but in a less categorical manner.

Spitz, R. (1972). Bridges: on anticipation, duration and meaning. *Journal of the American Psychoanalytic Association* 20:721–735.

A basic, conceptual paper on the epigenesis of bridging phenomena. Spitz places Winnicott in an even wider developmental perspective than Winnicott does himself.

Stevenson, O. (1954). The first treasured possession. *Psychoanalytic Study of the Child* 9:199–217. New York: International Universities Press.

An early study of the transitional object that has become one of the classics in the Winnicottian literature.

Ticho, E. (1974). Donald Winnicott, Martin Buber, and the theory of personal relationships. *Psychiatry* 37:240–253.

For those interested in the philosophical, religious, and existential aspects of Winnicott's work, this early paper on Buber and Winnicott should prove well worth reading.

Tolpin, M. (1971). On the beginning of a cohesive self: an application of the concept of transmuting internalization to the study of the transitional object and signal anxiety. *Psychoanalytic Study of the Child* 26:316–354. New Haven, CT: Yale University Press.

An important study that showed that, contrary to Winnicott, the transitional object did not just fade away but does become internalized into psychic structure. Also, one of the first attempts to correlate the ideas of Winnicott and Kohut.

Turner, J. (1988). Wordsworth and Winnicott in the area of play. *International Journal of Psycho-Analysis* 15:481–497.

An informed, fascinating literary comparison of the ideas on aesthetics of Winnicott, Wordsworth, and Coleridge.

Volkan, V. (1972). The linking objects of pathological mourners. *Archives of General Psychiatry* 27:215–225.

A good exposition of Volkan's helpful concept of the linking object (a memento of the deceased), which is used by the pathological mourner in a manner reminiscent of, but different from, the use of the transitional object to substitute for object loss.

References

Adler, G. (1989). Transitional phenomena, projective identification, and the essential ambiguity of the psychoanalytic situation. *Psychoanalytic Quarterly* 58:81–104.

Applebee, A. (1978). *The Child's Concept of Story: Ages Two to Seventeen.* Chicago: University of Chicago Press.

Arlow, J. (1969). Unconscious fantasy and disturbances of conscious experience. *Psychoanalytic Quarterly* 38:28–51.

Balint, M. (1968). *The Basic Fault: Therapeutic Aspects of Regression.* New York: Brunner/Mazel.

Bergman, A. (1978). From mother to the world outside: the use of space during the separation-individuation phase. In *Between Reality and Fantasy: Transitional Objects and Phenomena,* ed. S. Grolnick, L. Barkin, in collaboration with W. Muensterberger, pp. 145–165. Northvale, NJ: Jason Aronson.

Bettelheim, B. (1983). *Freud and Man's Soul.* New York: Alfred A. Knopf.

Brody, S. (1980). Transitional objects: idealization of a phenomenon. *Psychoanalytic Quarterly* 49:561–605.

Bruner, J., Jolly, A., and Sylva, K., eds. (1976). *Play: Its Role in Development and Evolution.* New York: Basic Books.

Busch, F. (1974). Dimensions of the first transitional object. *Psychoanalytic*

Study of the Child 29:215–229. New Haven, CT: Yale University Press.

Callois, R. (1958). *Man, Play and Games.* New York: The Free Press of Glencoe, 1961.

Cassirer, E. (1944). *An Essay on Man.* New Haven, CT: Yale University Press, 1965.

Cope, J. (1973). *The Theater and the Dream: From Metaphor to Form in Renaissance Drama.* Baltimore: The Johns Hopkins University Press.

Deri, S. (1978). Transitional phenomena: vicissitudes of symbolization and creativity. In *Between Reality and Fantasy: Transitional Objects and Phenomena,* ed. S. Grolnick, L. Barkin, in collaboration with W. Muensterberger, pp. 43–60. Northvale, NJ: Jason Aronson.

_____ (1984). *Symbolization and Creativity.* New York: International Universities Press.

Derrida, J. (1974). *Of Grammatology.* Baltimore: The Johns Hopkins University Press.

Ekecranz, L., and Ruhde, L. (1971). Transitional phenomena: frequency, form and functions of specifically loved objects. *Acta Psychiatrica Scandinavica* 48:261–273.

Emde, R. (1983). The prerepresentational self and its affective core. *Psycho-analytic Study of the Child* 38:165–192. New Haven, CT: Yale University Press.

Empson, W. (1930). *Seven Types of Ambiguity.* 3rd ed. Norfolk, VA: New Directions Books, 1953.

Erikson, E. (1950). *Childhood and Society.* New York: W. W. Norton.

Ferenczi, S. (1913). Stages in the development of the sense of reality. In *Sex in Psychoanalysis,* pp. 181–203. New York: Dover Publications, 1956.

Fraiberg, S. (1969). Libidinal object constancy and mental representation. *Psychoanalytic Study of the Child* 24:9–47. New York: International Universities Press.

Freud, S. (1905). Three essays on the theory of sexuality. *Standard Edition* 7:123–243. London: The Hogarth Press and the Institute of Psycho-Analysis.

_____ (1910). Leonardo Da Vinci and a memory of his childhood. *Standard Edition* 11:59–138.

_____ (1923). The ego and the id. *Standard Edition* 19:1–62.

Friedman, L. (1988). The clinical popularity of object relations concepts. *Psychoanalytic Quarterly* 57:667–691.

Gaddini, R. (1978). Transitional object origins and the psychosomatic symptom. In *Between Reality and Fantasy: Transitional Objects and Phenomena,* ed. S. Grolnick, L. Barkin, in collaboration with W. Muensterberger, pp. 109–131. Northvale, NJ: Jason Aronson.

Galenson, E., and Roiphe, H. (1971). The impact of early sexual discovery on mood, defensive organization, and symbolization. *Psychoanalytic Study of the Child* 26:195–216. New Haven, CT: Yale University Press.

Gesell, A. (1954) The ontogenesis of behavior. In *Manual of Child Psychology,* ed. L. Carmichael, pp. 335–373. New York: Wiley.

Giovacchini, P., ed. (1972). *Tactics and Techniques in Psychoanalytic Therapy.* New York: Science House.

Green, A. (1978). Potential space in psychoanalysis: the object in the setting. In *Between Reality and Fantasy: Transitional Objects and Phenomena,* ed. S. Grolnick, L. Barkin, in collaboration with W. Muensterberger, pp. 167–189. Northvale, NJ: Jason Aronson.

Greenacre, P. (1958). The family romance of the artist. *Psychoanalytic Study of the Child* 13:37–43. New York: International Universities Press.

Greenberg, J., and Mitchell, S. (1983). *Object Relations in Pyschoanalytic Theory.* Cambridge, MA: Harvard University Press.

Grolnick, S. (1978). Dreams and dreaming as transitional phenomena. In *Between Reality and Fantasy: Transitional Objects and Phenomena,* ed. S. Grolnick, L. Barkin, in collaboration with W. Muensterberger, pp. 213–231. Northvale, NJ: Jason Aronson.

_____ (1982). The current psychoanalytic dialogue: its counterpart in Renaissance philosophy. *Journal of the American Psychoanalytic Association* 30:679–699.

_____ (1984). Play, myth, theater and psychoanalysis. *Psychoanalytic Review* 71:247–262.

_____ (1986). The relationship of Winnicott's developmental concept of the transitional object to self and object constancy: clinical and theoretical perspectives. In *Self and Object Constancy,* ed. R. Lax, S. Bach, and J. Burland. New York: Guilford.

_____ (1987). A Winnicottian view of Mahler's concept of self and object constancy. Presented at an International Conference on Winnicott: *D. W. Winnicott and the Objects of Psychoanalysis.* Amherst, MA, June 12, 1987.

Grolnick S., Barkin, L., in collaboration with Muensterberger, W., eds. (1978). *Between Reality and Fantasy: Transitional Objects and Phenomena.* Northvale, NJ: Jason Aronson.

Grolnick, S., and Lengyel, A. (1978). Etruscan burial symbols and the transitional process. In *Between Reality and Fantasy: Transitional Objects and Phenomena,* ed. S. Grolnick, L. Barkin, in collaboration with W. Muensterberger, pp. 381–410. Northvale, NJ: Jason Aronson.

Groos, K. (1910). *The Play of Man.* New York: D. Appleton, 1914.

Grosskurth, P. (1986). *Klein: Her Work and Her Life.* New York: Alfred A. Knopf.

Hegel, G. (1830). *The Philosophy of History.* New York: Wiley, 1944.

Hirsch, E. (1967). *Validity in Interpretation.* New Haven, CT: Yale University Press.

Hodges, D. (1987). D. W. Winnicott and maternal metaphors. Presented at an International Conference on Winnicott: *D. W. Winnicott and the Objects of Psychoanalysis,* Amherst, MA, June 14, 1987.

Holland, N. (1975). *Five Readers Reading.* New Haven, CT: Yale University Press.

Holroyd, M. (1973). *Unreceived Opinions.* New York: Holt, Rinehart and Winston.

Hook, S., ed. (1959). *Psychoanalysis, Scientific Method and Philosophy.* New York: New York University Press.

Huizinga, J. (1955). *Homo Ludens: A Study of the Play Element in Culture.* Boston: Beacon Press.

Jacobson, E. (1964). *The Self and the Object World.* New York: International Universities Press.

Jakobson, R. (1960). Linguistics and poetics. In *Style and Language,* ed. T. Sebeok, pp. 350–377. Cambridge, MA: M.I.T. Press.

Kandel, E. (1978). Psychotherapy and the single synapse. *New England Journal of Medicine* 301:1028–1037.

Kernberg, O. (1975). *Borderline Conditions and Pathological Narcissism.* Northvale, NJ: Jason Aronson.

Kestenberg, J. (1971). From organ-object imagery to self and object representations. In *Separation-Individuation,* pp. 75–99. New York: International Universities Press.

Kestenberg, J., and Weinstein, J. (1978). Transitional objects and body-image formation. In *Between Reality and Fantasy: Transitional Objects and Phenomena,* ed. S. Grolnick, L. Barkin, in collaboration with W. Muensterberger, pp. 75–95. Northvale, NJ: Jason Aronson.

Khan, M. (1974). *The Privacy of the Self.* New York: International Universities Press.

Kirschenblatt-Gimblett, B., ed. (1976). *Speech Play: Research and Resources for the Study of Linguistic Creativity.* Philadelphia: University of Pennsylvania Press.

Klein, M. (1932). *The Psycho-analysis of Children.* New York: Grove Press, 1960.

Koestler, A. (1967). *The Ghost in the Machine.* Chicago: Henry Regnery.

Kohut, H. (1971). *The Analysis of the Self.* New York: International Universities Press.

Lacan, J. (1977). *Écrits: A Selection,* tr. Alan Sheridan. New York: Norton.

Langer, S. (1942). *Philosophy in a New Key.* Cambridge, MA: Harvard University Press, 1973.

Loewald, H. (1960). On the therapeutic action of psychoanalysis. *International Journal of Psycho-Analysis* 58:463–472.

_____ (1975). Psychoanalysis as an art and the fantasy character of the psychoanalytic situation. *Journal of the American Psychoanalytic Association* 23:227–299.

Lorenzer, A., and Orban, P. (1978). Transitional objects and phenomena: socialization and symbolization. In *Between Reality and Fantasy: Transitional Objects and Phenomena,* ed. S. Grolnick, L. Barkin, in collaboration with W. Muensterberger, pp. 471–482. Northvale, NJ: Jason Aronson.

Mack, J. (1965). Nightmares, conflict and ego development in childhood. *International Journal of Psycho-Analysis* 46:403–428.

Mahler, M., Pine, F., and Bergman, A. (1975). *The Psychological Birth of the Human Infant: Separation and Individuation.* New York: Basic Books.

Mahony, P. (1982). *Freud as a Writer.* New York: International Universities Press.

McDougall, J. (1982). *Theaters of the Mind.* New York: Basic Books, 1985.

Meisel, P., and Kendrick, W., eds. (1985). *Bloomsbury/Freud: The Letters of James and Alix Strachey. 1924–1925.* New York: Basic Books.

Meissner, W. (1984). *Psychoanalysis and Religion.* New Haven, CT: Yale University Press.

Merleau-Ponty, M. (1968). *The Visible and the Invisible.* Evanston, IL: Northwestern University Press.

Metcalf, D., and Spitz, R. (1978). The transitional object: critical developmental period and organizer of the psyche. In *Between Reality and Fantasy: Transitional Objects and Phenomena,* ed. S. Grolnick, L. Barkin, in collaboration with W. Muensterberger, pp. 99–108. Northvale, NJ: Jason Aronson.

Milner, M. (1978). D. W. Winnicott and the two-way journey. In *Between Reality and Fantasy: Transitional Objects and Phenomena,* ed. S.

Grolnick, L. Barkin, in collaboration with W. Muensterberger. Northvale, NJ: Jason Aronson.

Muensterberger, W. (1976). Personal communication.

Ornston, D. (1985). Freud's concept is different from Strachey's. *Journal of the American Psychoanalytic Association* 33:379–412.

Pedder, J. (1977). The role of space and location in psycho-analytic therapy, play and theater. *International Review of Psycho-Analysis* 4:215–224.

Phillips, A. (1988). *Winnicott.* London: Fontana Press. Also published by Harvard University Press.

Pine, F. (1988). The four psychologies of psychoanalysis and their place in clinical work. *Journal of the American Psychoanalytic Association* 36:571–596.

Rank, O. (1914). *The Double: A Psychoanalytic Study.* Chapel Hill, NC: University of North Carolina Press.

Rizzuto, A. (1981). *The Birth of the Living God: A Psychoanalytic Study.* Chicago: University of Chicago Press.

Rodman, F., ed. (1987). *The Spontaneous Gesture: Selected Letters of D. W. Winnicott.* Cambridge, MA: Harvard University Press.

Rose, G. (1978). The creativity of everyday life. In *Between Reality and Fantasy: Transitional Objects and Phenomena,* ed. S. Grolnick, L. Barkin, in collaboration with W. Muensterberger. Northvale, NJ: Jason Aronson.

_____ (1980). *The Power of Form: A Psychoanalytic Approach to Aesthetic Form.* New York: International Universities Press.

Rousseau, J. (1762). *Émile.* New York: Dutton, 1972.

Rycroft, C. (1985). *Psychoanalysis and Beyond.* Chicago: University of Chicago Press.

Sand, G. (1854). Histoire de Ma Vie. In *Studies of Childhood,* ed. James Sully, tr. M. Jöel, pp. 489–513. London: Longmans, Green and Co., 1906.

Sartre, J. (1953). *Existential Psychoanalysis.* Chicago: Henry Regnery.

Schacht, L. (1988). Winnicott's position in regard to the self with special reference to childhood. *International Review of Psycho-Analysis* 15:515–529.

Schafer, R. (1976). *A New Language for Psychoanalysis.* New Haven, CT: Yale University Press.

_____ (1983). *The Analytic Attitude.* New York: Basic Books.

Schiller, F. (1795). *On the Aesthetic Education of Man in a Series of Letters.* New York: Frederick Ungar, 1965.

Schneiderman, S., ed. (1980) *Returning to Freud: Clinical Psychoanalysis in the School of Lacan.* New Haven, CT: Yale University Press.

Schwartz, M. (1978). Critic define thyself. In *Pyschoanalysis and the Question of the Text,* ed. G. Hartman, pp. 1–17. Baltimore, MD: Johns Hopkins University Press.

Searles, H. (1960). *The Non-human Environment.* New York: International Universities Press.

Sechehaye, M. (1951). *Symbolic Realization: A New Method of Psychotherapy Applied to a Case of Schizophrenia.* Tr. B. Wursten and H. Wursten. New York: International Universities Press.

Segal H. (1957). Notes on symbol formation. *International Journal of Psycho-Analysis* 38:391–397.

———— (1975). *Introduction to the Work of Melanie Klein.* London: The Hogarth Press.

Slipp, S. (1984). *Object Relations: A Dynamic Bridge Between Individual and Family Treatment.* Northvale, NJ: Jason Aronson.

Spence, D. (1982). *Narrative Truth and Historical Truth: Meaning and Interpretation in Psychoanalysis.* New York: W. W. Norton.

Sperling, M. (1963). Fetishism in children. *Psychoanalytic Quarterly* 32:374–392.

Stern, D. (1985) *The Interpersonal World of the Infant: A View from Psychoanalysis and Developmental Psychology.* New York: Basic Books.

Stone, L. (1954). The widening scope of indications for psychoanalysis. *Journal of the American Psychoanalytic Association* 2:567–594.

Strachey, J. (1934). On the nature of the therapeutic action of psychoanalysis. *International Journal of Psycho-Analysis* 15:427–459.

Sully, J. (1906). *Studies of Childhood.* London: Longmans, Green and Co.

Sutherland, J. (1980). The British object relations theorists: Balint, Winnicott, Fairbairn, Guntrip. *Journal of the American Psychoanalytic Association* 28:829–860.

Ticho, E. (1974). Donald W. Winnicott, Martin Buber and the theory of personal relationships. *Psychiatry* 37:240–253.

Tolpin, M. (1971). On the beginnings of a cohesive self: an application of the concept of transmuting internalization to the study of the transitional object and signal anxiety. *Psychoanalytic Study of the Child* 26:316–354. New Haven, CT: Yale University Press.

Turner, J. (1988). Wordsworth and Winnicott in the area of play. *International Review of Psycho-Analysis* 15:481–497.

Volkan, V. (1973). Transitional fantasies in the analysis of a narcissistic personality. *Journal of the American Psychoanalytic Association* 21:351–376.

von Bertalanffy, L. (1933). *Modern Theories of Development.* London: Oxford University Press.

Weich, M. (1968). Language and object relations: towards the development of language constancy. Presented at the fall meeting of the American Psychoanalytic Association, December 21, 1968.

_____ (1978). Transitional language. In *Between Reality and Fantasy: Transitional Objects and Phenomena,* ed. S. Grolnick, L. Barkin, in collaboration with W. Muensterberger, pp. 413–423. Northvale, NJ: Jason Aronson.

Wentworth, H., and Flexner, S. (1960). *Dictionary of American Slang.* New York: Thomas Y. Crowell.

Werner, H., and Kaplan, B. (1963). *Symbol Formation.* New York: Wiley.

Winnicott, C. (1978). D. W. W.: a reflection. In *Between Reality and Fantasy: Transitional Objects and Phenomena,* ed. S. Grolnick, L. Barkin, in collaboration with W. Muensterberger, pp. 17–33. Northvale, NJ: Jason Aronson.

Winnicott, D. W. (1941). The observation of infants in a set situation. In *Collected Papers: Through Paediatrics to Psycho-analysis,* pp. 52–69. New York: Basic Books, 1958.

_____ (1945). Primitive emotional development. In *Collected Papers: Through Paediatrics to Psycho-analysis,* pp. 145–156. New York: Basic Books, 1958.

_____ (1947). Hate in the countertransference. In *Collected Papers: Through Paediatrics to Psycho-analysis,* pp. 194–203. New York: Basic Books, 1958.

_____ (1949). Mind and its relation to the psyche-soma. In *Collected Papers: Through Paediatrics to Psycho-analysis,* pp. 243–254. New York: Basic Books, 1958.

_____ (1951). Transitional objects and transitional phenomena. In *Collected Papers: Through Paediatrics to Psycho-analysis,* pp. 229–242. New York: Basic Books, 1958.

_____ (1955). Clinical varieties of transference. In *Collected Papers: Through Paediatrics to Psycho-analysis,* pp. 295–299. New York: Basic Books, 1958.

_____ (1956a). The antisocial tendency. In *Collected Papers: Through Paediatrics to Psycho-analysis,* pp. 306–315. New York: Basic Books, 1958.

_____ (1956b). Primary maternal preoccupation. In *Collected Papers:*

Through Paediatrics to Psycho-analysis, pp. 300–305. New York: Basic Books, 1958.

_____ (1957). Knowing and learning. In *Babies and Their Mothers.* Reading, PA: Addison-Wesley, 1987.

_____ (1958). The capacity to be alone. In *The Maturational Processes and the Facilitating Environment,* pp. 29–36. New York: International Universities Press, 1965.

_____ (1960a). Counter-transference. In *The Maturational Processes and the Facilitating Environment,* pp. 158–165. New York: International Universities Press, 1965.

_____ (1960b). Ego distortion in terms of true and false self. In *The Maturational Processes and the Facilitating Environment,* pp. 140–152. New York: International Universities Press, 1965.

_____ (1960c). On security. In *The Family and Individual Development,* pp. 30–33. London: Tavistock.

_____ (1960d). The theory of the parent–infant relationship. In *The Maturational Processes and the Facilitating Environment,* pp. 37–55. New York: International Universities Press, 1965.

_____ (1962). Ego integration in child development. In *The Maturational Processes and the Facilitating Environment,* pp. 56–63. New York: International Universities Press, 1965.

_____ (1963a). Communicating and not communicating leading to a study of certain opposites. In *The Maturational Processes and the Facilitating Environment,* pp. 179–192. New York: International Universities Press, 1965.

_____ (1963b). The development of the capacity for concern. In *The Maturational Processes and the Facilitating Environment,* pp. 73–82. New York: International Universities Press, 1965.

_____ (1963c). From dependence towards independence in the development of the individual. In *The Maturational Processes and the Facilitating Environment,* pp. 83–92. New York: International Universities Press, 1965.

_____ (1963d). Morals and education. In *The Maturational Processes and the Facilitating Environment,* pp. 93–105. New York: International Universities Press, 1965.

_____ (1964a). The baby as a person. In *The Child, the Family and the Outside World,* pp. 75–79. Harmondsworth: Penguin Books.

_____ (1964b). Further thoughts on babies as persons. In *The Child, the Family and the Outside World,* pp. 85–92. Harmondsworth: Penguin Books.

_____ (1964c). The innate morality of the baby. In *The Child, the Family and the Outside World*, pp. 93–97. Harmondsworth: Penguin Books.

_____ (1964d). Introduction. In *The Child, the Family and the Outside World*, pp. 9–11. Harmondsworth: Penguin Books.

_____ (1964e). This feminism. In *Home Is Where We Start from: Essays by a Psychoanalyst*, ed. C. Winnicott, R. Shepherd, and M. Davis, pp. 183–194. New York: W. W. Norton.

_____ (1965). *The Maturational Processes and the Facilitating Environment*. New York: International Universities Press.

_____ (1966). The ordinary devoted mother. In *Babies and Their Mothers*, pp. 1–14. Reading, PA: Addison-Wesley, 1987.

_____ (1968). Communication between infant and mother, and mother and infant, compared and contrasted. In *Babies and Their Mothers*, ed. C. Winnicott, R. Shepherd, and M. Davis, pp. 89–103. Reading, PA: Addison-Wesley, 1987.

_____ (1969). The mother–infant experience of mutuality. In *Parenthood: Its Psychology and Psychopathology*, ed. E. Anthony and T. Benedek. Boston: Little Brown.

_____ (1971a) Dreaming, fantasying and living. In *Playing and Reality*, pp. 26–37. New York: Basic Books.

_____ (1971b). The mirror-role of mother and family in child development. In *Playing and Reality*, pp. 111–118. New York: Basic Books.

_____ (1971c) *Playing and Reality*. New York: Basic Books.

_____ (1971d). *Therapeutic Consultations in Child Psychiatry*. New York: Basic Books.

_____ (1971e) The use of an object and relating through identifications. In *Playing and Reality*, pp. 86–94. New York: Basic Books.

_____ (1974). Fear of breakdown. *International Review of Psycho-Analysis* 1:103–107.

_____ (1977). *The Piggle: Account of the Psychoanalytic Treatment of a Little Girl*. New York: International Universities Press.

_____ (1986). *Holding and Interpretation: Fragment of an Analysis*. New York: Grove Press.

_____ (1987). *Babies and Their Mothers*. Reading, PA: Addison-Wesley.

_____ (1988). The concept of health using instinct theory. In *Human Nature*, pp. 51–64. New York: Schocken.

Wurmser, L. (1976). A defense of the use of metaphor in psychoanalytic theory formation. *Psychoanalytic Quarterly* 46:466–498.

Wylie, P. (1942). *Generation of Vipers*. New York: Farrar and Rinehart.

Young-Bruehl, E. (1988). *Anna Freud: A Biography*. New York: Summit Books.

Index

217